Poetry at One Remove

## POETS ON POETRY

**David Lehman, General Editor**
**Donald Hall, Founding Editor**

*New titles*

John Koethe, *Poetry at One Remove*
Yusef Komunyakaa, *Blue Notes*
Alicia Suskin Ostriker, *Dancing at the Devil's Party*

*Recently published*

Thom Gunn, *The Occasions of Poetry*
Edward Hirsch, *Responsive Reading*
John Hollander, *The Poetry of Everyday Life*
Philip Larkin, *Required Writing*
Geoffrey O'Brien, *Bardic Deadlines*
James Tate, *The Route as Briefed*

*Also available are collections by*

A. R. Ammons, Robert Bly, Philip Booth, Marianne Boruch,
Hayden Carruth, Fred Chappell, Amy Clampitt, Tom Clark,
Douglas Crase, Robert Creeley, Donald Davie, Peter Davison,
Tess Gallagher, Suzanne Gardinier, Allen Grossman, Thom Gunn,
John Haines, Donald Hall, Joy Harjo, Robert Hayden,
Daniel Hoffman, Jonathan Holden, Andrew Hudgins,
Josephine Jacobsen, Weldon Kees, Galway Kinnell, Mary Kinzie,
Kenneth Koch, Richard Kostelanetz, Maxine Kumin,
Martin Lammon (editor), David Lehman, Philip Levine,
John Logan, William Logan, William Matthews, William Meredith,
Jane Miller, Carol Muske, John Frederick Nims, Gregory Orr,
Marge Piercy, Anne Sexton, Charles Simic, Louis Simpson,
William Stafford, Anne Stevenson, May Swenson,
Richard Tillinghast, Diane Wakoski, C. K. Williams,
Alan Williamson, Charles Wright, and James Wright

*John Koethe*

# Poetry at
# One Remove
## ESSAYS

Ann Arbor

**THE UNIVERSITY OF MICHIGAN PRESS**

2003   2002   2001   2000      4   3   2   1

*A CIP catalog record for this book is available from the British Library.*

Library of Congress Cataloging-in-Publication Data

Koethe, John, 1945–
    Poetry at one remove : essays /John Koethe.
       p.   cm. — (Poets on poetry)
    Includes bibliographical references (p.).
    ISBN 0-472-09709-1 (alk. paper)
    ISBN 0-472-06709-5 (pbk. : alk. paper)
    1. Koethe, John, 1945–   —Aesthetics.   2. Poetry—History
and criticism—Theory, etc.   3. Philosophy in literature.
4. Poetics.   I. Title.   II. Series.
PS3561.O35P64   1999
809.1—dc21                                        99-6806
                                                       CIP

*To Douglas Crase*

# Contents

# Introduction

## *Poetry and the Structure of Speculation*

As a poet who is also a philosopher, I've long had a sense that some sort of kinship, however indirect, exists between these two forms of activity in which the mind becomes engaged through the medium of language. But at the same time I've also been unsure, and continue to be unsure, exactly what that kinship might be. The essays in this book do not attempt to offer an account of the relationship between poetry and philosophy (assuming there is one); rather, they manifest my sense that some of the themes and habits of thought that have a place in the latter discipline can find a home in the former as well.

Plato famously denied poetry a place in his ideal city, a denial made all the more poignant by the fact that he himself had written poetry in his youth and, through his philosophical writings, ranks as one of the Western canon's greatest stylists (surely Socrates' death scene in the *Phaedo* is one of the most moving depictions to be found in imaginative literature). But his reasons for banishing poetry from the republic are actually indicative of a certain affinity between it and philosophy, at least at the level of content if not of purpose. Plato feared that poetry's rhythmic and metrical qualities—or, put more broadly, its affective dimension—might lead it to rival or displace philosophy as the basis on which the city would be governed, even though the poet's relation to his subject matter was not one of knowledge or even informed opinion. Yet this fear indicates that Plato thought that poetry and philosophy could at least appear to share certain themes and ideas—for otherwise how could what he regarded as poetry's ill-founded pronouncements threaten the authority of philosophy's properly grounded claims? Plato's opposition to poetry is thus based on a grudging respect for it and a recognition that poetry and philosophy have enough in common for there to be a danger of one being mistaken for the other.

Many poets and readers of poetry hold what seems to me to be an overly narrow view of its range and possibilities, one that insists on the concrete and particular and proscribes the abstract and discursive. Such a view strikes me as pernicious, and I try to counter it in one of these essays, "Poetry and the Experience of Experience." But though I think that poetry ought to be open to the kind of theoretical reflection we associate with philosophy, it isn't at all clear to me just what philosophy can actually bring to it. Few poets, even those of a meditative bent, have had any formal training in the discipline (to my knowledge, there is only one other active and established poet who is also a philosopher); and the idea of investing poetry with doctrines and arguments taken wholesale from academic philosophy is repugnant to me. One advantage of a philosophical background is that it makes one at ease with the discursive and with the rhetoric of abstraction, which of course are philosophy's stock in trade. Eliot was one of the few poets actually trained in the discipline, as Stevens was not. And I think that this difference is manifested in their writings. For all the magnificence of his major meditations, there are times (fortunately rare) when Stevens's theoretical ruminations seem a bit forced, and a note of posturing creeps in. Eliot, in his late meditations—in *Four Quartets,* say—seems to me to venture into the realm of abstraction with greater assurance, and his deployment of the language of the intellect always seems limpid and matter-of-fact even at its most rarified.

I think that poetry and philosophy are both speculative activities, in that both involve the entertainment of propositions in the absence of certainty about their truth and often in the absence of any means of even establishing their truth. And if one rejects the narrow view of poetry that limits it to the concrete and personal, the propositions they involve may be, in a broad sense, similar in kind. Yet the structures of speculation they each involve seem to me quite different. I remember a conversation in graduate school in which Rogers Albritton, a philosopher legendary for his caution and tenacity, remarked, in a variation of Eliot's line, "There in the footnotes I feel free." The point of course is that speculation in philosophy is essentially constrained in the way it develops and proceeds. It is typically initiated by the recognition of a *problem,* usually not a problem first formulated by the philosopher himself but one that has previously been raised and discussed by others, who have ventured various solutions to it. One then proceeds to canvass these solutions, to defend one of them or to offer objections that render them untenable, and then perhaps to put forward for consideration a new proposal, to be critically examined in turn. This process is constrained both in its inception and its development: positions have to be offered in response to recognized problems, and once objections to a position have been adduced one can't continue to maintain the position until those objections have been rebutted (though of course one may register one's intuition that the position is in fact correct, even though one isn't sure how to answer the objections to it).

Speculation in poetry is, by contrast, unconstrained, or at least not subject to the same kind of constraints, and the way it is initiated and proceeds seems to me to have a very different structure. Coleridge's remark about "the willing suspension of disbelief that constitutes poetic faith" is directed at the relation of the reader to the poem and posits a more or less passive abandonment of ordinary standards of plausibility. But I think that something like a more active form of this relation holds between the *poet* and the poem, where the aim is the creation, through an act of will, of an extraordinary construction, which may be personal or impersonal, abstract or concrete. The occasion is typically a heightened awareness of a situation or one-self, and in the course of the poem's elaboration one may entertain and essay notions of whose untenability one is perfectly aware—an untenability one may even acknowledge—without being led to abandon them. Indeed the awareness of the futility of a conception may lead to an even greater insistence on it, because the animating force of poetic speculation is always *desire,* rather than an ideal of impersonal accuracy.

Theses and concepts, explanations and hypotheses, seem to me to enter into poetry more as possibilities to be explored and inhabited (as opposed to being assessed and evaluated), and the poet, if he finds the habitation congenial, isn't likely to abandon them simply because the property has been declared condemned.

Stevens begins "Notes toward a Supreme Fiction"—and of course the title is already an acknowledgment—by registering his location at the center of the poetic imagination:

> In the uncertain light of a single, certain truth,
> Equal in living changingness to the light
> In which I meet you, in which we sit at rest,
> For a moment of the central of our being.

He proceeds to define the dimensions of that imagination through a series of injunctions—*It Must Be Abstract, It Must Change, It Must Give Pleasure*—each of which, in its insistence, plants seeds of its own undoing. The impulse is to conceive of the world as pure form—"The inconceivable idea of the sun"—prior to its disappointing actualization in the familiar:

> You must become an ignorant man again
> And see the sun again with an ignorant eye
> And see it clearly in the idea of it.

Yet the cleanliness of this "first idea" is threatened by the "poisonous . . . ravishments of truth, so fatal to / The truth itself," which lead to "an ennui of the first idea." Stevens associates the threat posed by an insistence on truth with philosophy, which he says is animated by a desire occasioned by a concomitant lack: "The philosopher desires. // And not to have is the beginning of desire." The impetus of the poetic imagination, he insists, is different:

> The romantic intoning, the declaimed clairvoyance
> Are parts of apotheosis, appropriate
> And of its nature, the idiom thereof.
>
> They differ from reason's click-clack, its applied
> Enflashings.

Yet though this "romantic intoning" may be "the idiom thereof," it is not "The origin of the major man" of the imagination, which is rather ". . . the object of // The hum of thoughts evaded in the mind." Stevens has it that the apprehension of the supreme fiction of the first idea of the world is the result not of an act of will but of passive receptivity:

> But to impose is not
> To discover. To discover an order as of
> A season, to discover summer and know it,
>
> To discover winter and know it well, to find,
> Not to impose, not to have reasoned at all,
> Out of nothing to have come on major weather.

Yet this evocation of the longed-for apprehension of reality through acquiescence is immediately followed by a remarkable outburst of desperate insistence that betrays his own disbelief:

> It is possible, possible, possible. It must
> Be possible. It must be that in time
> The real will from its crude compoundings come,
>
> Seeming, at first, a beast disgorged, unlike,
> Warmed by a desperate milk. To find the real,
> To be stripped of every fiction except one,
>
> The fiction of an absolute.

"What am I to believe?" the poet asks. But rather than abandon the vision in the face of the recognition of its unattainability, the poem moves towards its conclusion in a reaffirmation of "the more than rational distortion, / The fiction that results from feeling":

> They will get it straight one day at the Sorbonne.
> We shall return at twilight from the lecture
> Pleased that the irrational is rational,
> Until flicked by feeling, in a gildered street,
> I call you by name, my green, my fluent mundo.
> You will have stopped revolving except in crystal.

In Stevens the recognition of the futility of the poet's specu-
lation is usually not registered explicitly but is implied by a
willful and heightened insistence and the use of interroga-
tives. But in other poets the breaking of the poetic spell does
become explicit—for instance, in Keats's Nightingale ode:

> Forlorne! the very word is like a bell
>   To toll me back from thee to my sole self!
> Adieu! the fancy cannot cheat so well
>   As she is fam'd to do, deceiving elf.
> Adieu! adieu! thy plaintive anthem fades.

Or consider James Merrill's "Lost in Translation,"[1] which,
though not abstract and discursive in the way Stevens's poem
is, exhibits the same movement from elaboration to acknowl-
edgment of futility to reaffirmation I am trying to locate. The
poet's evocation of a childhood scene leads to an *apparent* mem-
ory of a translation by Rilke of Valery's "Palme," the search for
which remains in the background of his recollection of assem-
bling, as a child, an elaborate and fantastic puzzle, which is
then disassembled and collapses into nothingness: "The puz-
zle hung together—and did not." The fictive puzzle of child-
hood was capable of completion; but those belonging to the
poet's mature life are not—"so many later puzzles / Had miss-
ing pieces"—including the puzzle of Rilke's poem:

> I've spent the last days, furthermore,
> Ransacking Athens for that translation of "Palme."
> Neither the Goethehaus nor the National Library
> Seems able to unearth it. Yet I can't
> Just be imagining. I've seen it.

"Lost is it, buried? One more missing piece." Yet rather than
accept their unreality, the poem concludes with an oblique
declaration of the power of these missing pieces:

> But nothing's lost. Or else: all is translation
> And every bit of us is lost in it
> (Or found—I wonder through the ruins of S
> Now and then, wondering at the peacefulness)

And in that loss a self-effacing tree,
Color of context, imperceptibly
Rustling with its angel, turns the waste
To shade and fiber, milk and memory.

Let me offer Elizabeth Bishop's "Over 2,000 Illustrations and a Complete Concordance"[2] as a final example. A volume of engravings of foreign subjects initiates a reverie about what "should have been our travels" and leads to an induced recollection of the poet's actual travels, which are disconnected and demystified but which take on a specious narrative coherence as the recollection progresses; only to be deflated by the recognition of "Everything only connected by 'and' and 'and.' " Yet the poet then returns to the volume that initiated the process that led to this deflation—"Open the book"—and the poem concludes with an evocation of the still longed-for epiphany that her actual journeys have failed to disclose:

Open the heavy book. Why couldn't we have seen
this old Nativity while we were at it?
—the dark ajar, the rocks breaking with light,
an undisturbed, unbreathing flame,
colorless, sparkless, freely fed on straw,
and, lulled within, a family with pets,
—and looked and looked our infant sight away.

This theme of assertion in the face of futility surfaces repeatedly in the essays making up this book. Most of them are occasional pieces, written in response to requests or invitations. But it does seem to me, in retrospect, that something like a coherent view of poetry and mentality emerges from them. The prevailing theme is the way in which poetry attempts to situate subjectivity in relation to its objective setting in the world. At first this takes the form of reflections on how various conceptions of the self or subject inform the work of particular poets; but then it becomes a concern with subjective experience in a broader sense: how the affirmation of subjectivity is central to romanticism and to the major line of American poetry that descends from romanticism and how poetry tries to accomplish this affirmation by enacting something like the movements of what Kant called the dynamical sublime. There is also a continuing concern with how a poetry that attempts to accommodate subjective experience in its full generality is related to the discursive mode and to outlooks associated with philosophy and literary theory.

A number of these essays address the work of a particular poet, John Ashbery. Everything I've written here grows out of my own experience as a poet and my reflections on what is involved in writing poetry of the sort to which I aspire; and Ashbery (along with Stevens and Eliot) has been the dominant influence on my work. Moreover, the conception of romanticism that emerges from these pieces—of the affirmation of subjectivity through its contestation of its objective setting—is one that seems to me to be central to Ashbery's poetry (though some would probably dispute this), especially the poetry belonging to what I think of as his high meditative period, running roughly from *Rivers and Mountains* (1966) through *A Wave* (1984). Ashbery's work is also striking in the way it manages to maintain the tensions of romanticism within a loose and discursive framework, which is another theme running throughout this book.

The most considered essays here are "The Metaphysical Subject of John Ashbery's Poetry," "Contrary Impulses: The Tension between Poetry and Theory," "The Absence of a Noble Presence," "Poetry and the Experience of Experience," "The Romance of Realism," and "Poetry at One Remove." I've also included two pieces that were written as reviews ("Ashbery's Meditations" and "Prose Poems and Poet's Prose"), some remarks prepared for a conference ("The Subject of Extremity"), and two short appreciations of Joan Murray and James Schuyler. These prefigure some of the themes that take a more developed form in the succeeding essays and also broaden the range of poetic reference. I haven't included reviews that seemed to me to have no real implications beyond the books they discussed.

I make no pretense of being either a literary scholar or critic. What the pieces in this book amount to are the musings, by someone given to self-reflection, of a working poet who is also a philosopher. I hope the views they contain have some intrinsic interest; but beyond that I think their interest lies in the fact that, while the relation of poetry to philosophy is an intriguing and vexing one, there are, as I said earlier, few who actually engage in both activities. My aim in these essays has been less to defend positions and persuade others of them than to register certain connections between ideas, however vaguely formulated, that have seemed important to me in my own work. I've simply arranged them in chronological order (the dates given are those of composition) and left them, apart from a few minor corrections, as they were originally written.

Albritton's remark about the freedom one feels when one leaves the confines of formal philosophy was one I brought up earlier in connection with the difference between the way speculation is conducted in poetry and the way it figures in philosophy. But the unconstrained manner in which speculation proceeds in poetry also seems to me to be something like the one governing these reflections *about* poetry. At any rate, this is the spirit in which I feel they were written, and I hope they will be read in, and help sustain, that spirit.


NOTES

1. In James Merrill, *Divine Comedies* (New York: Atheneum, 1976).

2. In Elizabeth Bishop, *The Complete Poems, 1927–1979* (New York: Farrar, Straus and Giroux, 1983).

# Ashbery's Meditations
## (1972)

At first one feels that not many objects came into play; then one realizes that they were all there, only they went by so quickly:

> we must register our appraisal of the moving world that is around us, but our song is leading us on now, farther and farther into that wilderness and away from the shrouded but familiar forms that were its first inspiration.

Sometimes there is a kind of tunnel vision:

> a strange kind of happiness within the limitations. The way is narrow but it is not hard, it almost seems to propel or push one along. One gets the narrowness into one's seeing.

Then almost suddenly

> one wall of even radiance . . . open to the movements and suggestions of this new life of action without development, a fixed flame.

*Three Poems* (New York: Viking, 1972) plots that life that, after all, includes every other one, all "previous forms of life: the animalistic one, the aristocratic one," the "slow burst that narrows to a final release," "the ritual approach"; each relieved by "two kind of happiness . . . the frontal and the latent," and permeated by ideas, "some harebrained, others daringly original"; the whole thing "perfect in its vulgarity," like life itself.

From *Parnassus* (fall–winter 1972). Reprinted by permission.

On the other hand, it is also an exploration of that peculiar form of life we allow works of art, "placed over the real like a sheet of tracing paper," "the absorption of ourselves seen from the outside." But just how does this differ from the life we allow others, even our own? "They can join, but never touch"; and yet

> there is even a doubt as to our own existence. Why, after all, were we not destroyed in the conflagration of the moment our real and imaginary lives coincided, unless it was because we never had a separate existence.

The answer seems to be: our separate existence *is* that coincidence, which occurs every moment—

> until one day we wake up a different color, the color of the filter of the opinions and ideas everyone has ever entertained about us. And in this form we must prepare, now, to try to live.

But that is every day.

There are several misconceptions about John Ashbery's work. He is often considered an anomaly—"daringly original," to be sure, but ultimately a kind of prestidigitator with his bag of tricks. This usually takes the form of praise: his language is dense but mysteriously buoyant, he modulates it like a medium, and the logic of his poems is as invisible as it is hypnotic; finally, his entire work constitutes a sort of floating monument to itself, modernism's fullest flower. Versions of this view are held by both enthusiasts and detractors. Aside from its shallowness—since all that is true of virtually every great poet—it obscures the fact that one of the questions Ashbery takes most urgently is whether any expression can be adequate to the need that prompted it.

> Perhaps no art, however gifted and well-intentioned, can supply what we were demanding of it: not only the figured representation of our days but the justification of them, the reckoning and its application, so close to the reality being lived that it vanishes suddenly in a thunderclap, with a loud cry.

Looking at Ashbery's work in aesthetic terms alone makes about as much sense as taking Traherne's *Centuries of Meditation* (with which *Three Poems* has a great deal in common) as a response to the itch to meditate. *Of course* Ashbery is innovative; it is just beyond that point that his poetry begins.

> You know now the sorrow of continually doing something you cannot name, of producing automatically as an apple tree produces apples this thing there is no name for. And you continue to hum as you move forward, but your heart is pounding.

We might get a clearer view of it by abandoning the pretense that we already know what poems are and are in a position to recognize a (merely) new one. *Three Poems* almost forces us to abandon it. What they "are," after all, are *meditations*—which derivatively describes a form but primarily an activity

> which can only exist by coming into existence, and then the rules may be drawn up, though it makes very little difference since no one will ever play that game again.

And the essence of a meditation—Descartes's, Traherne's, Proust's, Ashbery's—is the urgent exploration (by whatever means available) of a recognizable, but until now unrecognized, problem; an exploration covering—or, rather, defining—a concrete stretch of human time:

> It must awaken from the sleep of being part of some other, old problem, and by that time its new problematic existence will have already begun, carrying it forward into situations with which it cannot cope, since no one recognizes it and it does not even recognize itself yet, or know what it is. It is like the beginning of a beautiful day.

*Three Poems* explicitly assumes the form; but all of Ashbery's works are meditations, and with that sort of necessity: "These things led into life." And yet: "This was not even the life that was going to happen to us." Which raises a question: *whose* lives are the ones floating in and out of these meditations? To which he seems to reply: yours and mine and others, of course; while at the same time "each of us is this multitude as well as that isolated individual." This is *one* road leading through the trilogy.

Suppose you had to give an account of the subject of your experiences that explained both why you *had* them and why you were distinct from them. Clearly you have to, since there is no "retreat to the death of childhood" where that question never arose. But just as clearly it is impossible to finish—even, almost, to begin—for, on the one hand, the subject constantly merges with its experiences, so that it loses identity; while, on the other, it retreats from them, so that it abandons all relation to the world in which it is supposed to live.

> But meanwhile I am to include everything: the furniture of this room, everyday expressions, as well as my rarest thoughts and dreams, so that you may never become aware of the scattered nature of it, and meanwhile you *are* it all.

> Perhaps what I am saying is that it is I the subject, recoiling from you at an ever-increasing rate of speed just so as to be able to say I exist in that safe vacuum . . . As if I were only a flower after all and not the map of the country in which it grows.

And from this standpoint (the only one imaginable) any knowledge of one's own existence—"the task of trying to revive those memories, make them real, as if to live again were the only reality"—is that of someone else's:

> any breathing is to be breathing into each other, and imperfect, like all apprehended things.

> In you I fall apart, and outwardly am a single fragment, a puzzle to itself.

> Therefore I hold you. But life holds us, and is unknowable.

For Ashbery art is an activity, *the* activity, leading to that knowledge: which is ultimately unattainable, not because it is, in an imaginable sense, ineffable—"All the facts are here and it remains only to use them in the right combinations"—but because that activity is inexhaustible, like the life in which it occurs. Finally it makes no difference that it constantly, as it happens, ceases; what matters is the ability

> to use the wings that could have saved us by bearing us aloft if only for a little distance, not the boundless leagues we had been hoping for and insisting on, but enough to make a crucial difference, the difference between life and death.

Against Ashbery's the work of most other poets seems dismally contingent. Somehow it is just the even weight he allows each thing, the possibility of blending "in a union too subtle to cause any comment," that accounts for its stature. This is a vision as simple to understand as it is impossible to learn.

# The Metaphysical Subject of
# John Ashbery's Poetry
## *(1978)*

A conception of the self can inform a poet's work in a variety of ways. Perhaps the most familiar is through its possession of a distinctive "voice," which basically amounts to a projection of a personality—either the poet's actual personality or one he assumes. There can be as many voices as there are personalities, but it does not follow that differences between two poets' voices reflect a difference in the *conception* of the self that informs their work. For example, Robert Lowell's characteristic voice is quite different from John Berryman's, and the personalities their poems project are correspondingly different. But it strikes me that these distinctive personalities represent selves of essentially the same *kind:* they *are* personalities, that is, they are or are to be regarded as actual psychological egos as much a part of the real world as the historical circumstances, incidents, feelings, and relationships with which they become engaged. Poetry that is characterized primarily by its voice embodies, it seems to me, a psychological conception of the self: the self is a real entity among other real entities, maybe more important than most of them, but, like them, a part of the world it is trying to tell us about.

But poetry can also involve conceptions of the self not so directly tied to the poet's own distinctive personality or voice. It can force us to consider the *position* of the "speaker"—or what I would prefer to call the "subject"—of the poetry with

From *Beyond Amazement: New Essays on John Ashbery,* ed. David Lehman (Ithaca: Cornell University Press, 1980). Reprinted by permission of Cornell University Press.

respect to the incidents, objects, thoughts, and personalities (including the poet's own) it describes. And sometimes this position seems drastically different from the vantage point in the world that the poem presents and that is occupied by the psychological subject of the poem. In reading poetry informed primarily by the psychological notion of the self embodied in the poet's voice, we are struck by questions like "How does he sound?" or "Whose voice is it?" (and a sense that the answers to these questions are indeterminate tells against the poetry). But for poetry involving a less psychological conception of the self or subject, the important question is not so much what the voice sounds like as *where it comes from;* and a mark of the success of this sort of poetry is that this question seems to *have* a determinate answer, even when we find ourselves unable to formulate it.

*Remembrance of Things Past* serves to illustrate the difference between the conceptions of a psychological ego and a nonpsychological subject. The character Marcel has a particular personality and lives *in* time and in tension between Swann's way of domesticity and the Guermantes' way of social circulation. And we can think of the novel as Marcel's autobiography, whose theme is the fusing of the two ways over the course of time. But the vantage point of the narrator is an atemporal one from which the moments in his life do not succeed one another but coexist simultaneously. We are supposed to read the novel twice, the second time not as autobiography but as the narrator's attempt to circumscribe the atemporal position Marcel comes to occupy at the end. Had someone other than Proust written a novel to this point, the personality of the protagonist and the incidents of his life would have been different: the psychological ego embodied in the work would not have been Marcel's. Yet the *subject* of this hypothetical novel could have been the same: a *different* voice could have emanated from the same durationless position occupied by Proust's narrator.

Now it seems to me that a distinctive quality of John Ashbery's poetry, a source of much of its power, is that the conception of the self it embodies is not primarily a psychological one. I say not *primarily* psychological, because his work *is* possessed of an authentic individual voice, gently reticent, delighting equally in the abstract, the literal, and the silly, and usually heard through a haze of humor:

> And so we too
> Came where the others came: nights of physical endurance,
> Or if, by day, our behavior was anarchically
> Correct, at least by New Brutalism standards, all then
> Grew taciturn by previous agreement. We were spirited
> Away *en bateau,* under cover of fudge dark.
> It's not the incomplete importunes, but the spookiness
> Of the finished product.
>
> ("Daffy Duck in Hollywood")[1]

This passage captures some of Ashbery's characteristic "twang." He does actually something like this in conversation, and one reason his imitators are usually unconvincing is that this tone, however cool and detached, works to project a genuine human voice and personality, in whose absence it seems (like any strong poet's style in someone else's mouth) willed, mannered, and depersonalized.

But even though Ashbery's work embodies the presence of a particular psychological ego, it is almost unique in the degree to which it is informed by a nonpsychological conception of the self or subject: a unitary consciousness from which his voice originates, positioned outside the temporal flux of thought and experience his poetry manages to monitor and record (*almost* unique in this respect: I sometimes feel something similar to be true of Elizabeth Bishop's work, though—and this is part of the point—her *voice* is decidedly different from his). The sense of the presence of a unified subject that conceives these poems is very strong, almost palpable. Among the stylistic indications that this subject is not a particular personality are Ashbery's characteristic use of pronouns: it seems a matter of indifference whether the subject is referred to as "I," "you," "he," "she," "it," or "we,"[2] shifts between which often occur rapidly within the course of the same poem:

## SHE

But now always from your plaint I
Relive, revive, springing up careless,
Dust geyser in city absentmindedness,
And all day it is writ and said:
We round women like corners. They are the friends
We were always saying goodbye to and then
Bumping into the next day. School has closed
Its doors on a few. Saddened, she rose up
And untwined the gears of that blank, blossoming day.
"So much for Paris, and the living in this world."
But I was going to say
It differently, about the way
Time is sorting us all out, keeping you and her
Together yet apart, in a give-and-take, push-pull
Kind of environment. And then, packed like sardines,
Our wit arises, survives automatically. We imbibe it.

This from "Fantasia on 'The Nut-Brown Maid,' "[3] a long
poem written in the form of a dialogue between HE and SHE,
two identities that are not really differentiated by the poem at
all. The references of *HE* and *SHE,* the pronouns within the
previous passage, and Ashbery's pronouns generally, are ana-
phoric. But these references are never given *in* the poem: they
seem to belong to a world outside it, and there is a strong
sense that any distinctions between them would be basically
arbitrary.

"Time is sorting us all out." Another stylistic clue to the
nature of Ashbery's subject is the pervasive sense of temporal
dislocation that characterizes his work: the grammatical past
tense is often used to indicate the present of the poem, even
when the present is the moment of writing itself (as David
Kalstone has observed, "Tense will shift while the poem refers
to itself as part of the past").[4] Another passage from "Fantasia"
both illustrates and offhandedly tries to explain this tendency:

## HE

To him, the holiday-making crowds were
Energies of a parallel disaster, the fulfilling
Of all prophecies between now and the day of

Judgment. Spiraling like fish,
Toward a distant, unperceived surface, was all
The reflection there was. Somewhere it had its opaque
Momentary existence.
      But if each act
Is reflexive, concerned with itself on another level
As well as with us, the strangers who live here,
Can one advance one step further without sinking equally
Far back into the past? There was always something to see,
Something going on, for the historical past owed it
To itself, our historical present. Another month a huge
Used-car sale on the lawn shredded the sense of much
Of the sun coming through the wires, or a cape
Would be rounded by a slim white sail almost
Invisible in the specific design, or children would come
Clattering down fire escapes until the margin
Exploded into an ear of sky. Today the hospitals
Are light, airy places, tented clouds, and the weeping
In corridors is like autumn showers. It's beginning.

Time's job of "sorting us all out" is always in progress but never gets completed, for the subject cannot "advance one step further without sinking equally / Far back into the past." Ashbery's subject seems possessed by an impulse, which it knows has to be frustrated, to *reify* itself, to find or create some *thing* with which it can identify totally:

I shall use my anger to build a bridge like that
Of Avignon, on which people may dance for the feeling
Of dancing on a bridge. I shall at last see my complete face
Reflected not in the water but in the worn stone floor of my
 bridge.

               ("Wet Casements")[5]

"I shall at last see"—the tone is wistful and resigned. The attempt at reification yields only a personality or image that is "other," "A portrait, smooth as glass . . . built up out of multiple corrections / [which] has no relation to the space or time in which it was lived" ("Definition of Blue").[6] The subject inhabits "the sigh of our present" ("Blue Sonata")[7] and is timeless, while any representative of it in the real world is time bound, part of "The present past of which our features, / Our opinions are made." It can only be a *surface:*

> But your eyes proclaim
> That everything is surface. The surface is what's there
> And nothing can exist except what's there.
>> ("Self-Portrait in a Convex Mirror")[8]

The note of desperation in the poetry that attends the subject's impulse to reify itself does not arise because the surface representation leaves out something real:

> there are no words for the surface, that is,
> No words to say what it really is, that it is not
> Superficial but a visible core.

This "Wooden and external representation / Returns the full echo of what you meant / With nothing left over" ("Clepsydra").[9] Rather, the trouble is that the subject and its "Wooden and external representation" occupy fundamentally different *positions.* The latter, like the psychological ego or self, *is* a thing, existing in the real world of past, present, and future; whereas the subject of Ashbery's poems—what I shall call the "metaphysical subject"—seems to inhabit a durationless "now," existing in a condition of "drifting . . . toward a surface which can never be approached, / Never pierced through into the timeless energy of a present" ("Wet Casements"). And what both drives and frustrates his poetry is the attempt to fuse the two positions, an attempt conducted in the full knowledge that it cannot possibly succeed: "Why, after all, were we not destroyed in the conflagration of the moment our real and imaginary lives coincided, unless it was because we never had a separate existence beyond those two static and highly artificial concepts whose fusion was nevertheless the cause of death and destruction not only for ourselves but in the world around us?" ("The Recital").[10]

At this point we might be tempted to conclude that the moral of Ashbery's work is that the whole concept of the self is delusory. This would be a mistake. It is true only to the extent that by "I" one understands an individual psychological ego or personality: the referential and temporal vagaries of his poetry are simply incompatible with the speaker's being a real person in the world, with a particular, individual biography. What is striking about Ashbery's work is that, despite these distortions and pressures to which his "self" is subjected, surely sufficient to dismantle any *personality,* one never loses the sense that a perfectly definite point of consciousness is behind the whole enterprise. Later I want to compare the concepts of the self that inform Ashbery's work and Frank O'Hara's: both of them try to undermine the notion of the self as a permanent and objective personality, but I think one (among many) of the significant differences between them involves the different philosophical conceptions of the self alternative to that of the psychological ego to which their works have affinities.

The reification of the self as the psychological ego represents what might be called a Cartesian conception of the self. According to this conception, the self *is* an object in the world among other objects (Descartes identifies it with the mind, a *res cogitans* or "thinking thing"); and as an object in the world we can experience it (introspectively), hold beliefs about it, and frame descriptions of it—at least as much as we can for any object in the world (e.g., the sun). Of course, for Descartes the mind or self is a spiritual or mental substance, unlike, say, the sun, which is a physical or material substance; but this just means that our world of acquaintance and experience contains substances of two sorts, mental and material, and does not affect the main point of this conception of the self—that it *is* a substance or thing and part of the world of substantial things.

Descartes's is not the only view of the self found in the Western philosophical tradition. Hume's critique of the Cartesian conception boils down to the idea that experience simply fails to acquaint us with any single persisting thing we might mean by "I" but, rather, discloses only the various sensations and passions we mistakenly ascribe to a persisting self whose experiences we take them to be:

> But self or person is not any one impression, but that to
> which our several impressions and ideas are supposed to have

reference. If any impression gives rise to the idea of self, that impression must continue invariably the same, thro' the whole course of our lives; since self is supposed to continue to exist after that manner. But there is no impression constant and invariable. Pain and pleasure, grief and joy, passions and sensations succeed each other, and never all exist at the same time . . . For my part, when I enter most intimately into what I call *myself,* I always stumble on some particular perception or other, of heat or cold, light or shade, love or hatred, pain or pleasure. I can never catch *myself* at any time without a perception, and never can observe anything but the perception . . . I may venture to affirm of . . . mankind, that they are nothing but a bundle or collection of different perceptions, which succeed each other with an inconceivable rapidity, and are in perpetual flux and movement.[11]

According to Hume's conception, there is literally *no such thing* as the self. The illusion that there is is partly grammatical and partly due to resemblances between the perceptions comprising the bundle. What is real are the perceptions themselves; but what is illusory is the persisting Cartesian ego whose perceptions we take them to be.

A third conception of the self derives from Kant and emerges in a somewhat modified form in Schopenhauer and Wittgenstein. Consciousness, Hume's "bundle of perceptions," possesses a unity that cannot be reduced to relations of resemblance among its constituents; but Descartes's error, according to Kant, consists in confusing this unity of conscious experience with the experience of a unitary substance, a self or subject. We can have no *concept* of such an ego, for to us it is "nothing more than the feeling of an existence without the least concept . . . only the representation of that to which all thinking stands in relation":[12]

We do not have, and cannot have, any knowledge whatsoever of any such subject. Consciousness is, indeed, that which alone makes all representations to be thoughts, and in it, therefore, as the transcendental subject, all our perceptions must be found; but beyond this logical meaning of the word "I," we have no knowledge of the subject in itself, which as substratum underlies this "I," as it does all thoughts.[13]

Schopenhauer's modification was to reify this purely logical notion of the transcendental ego yet to construe it not as a substantial thing in the world but "as an indivisible point" outside space and time,[14] on whose existence the world or experience and representation rests. And it is this somewhat murky conception of the self that lies behind Wittgenstein's obscure remarks towards the end of the *Tractatus:*

> I am my world. (The microcosm.)
> There is no such thing as the subject that thinks or entertains ideas.
> If I wrote a book called *The World as I found it,* I should have to include a report on my body, and should have to say what parts were subordinate to my will, and which were not, etc., this being a method of isolating the subject, or rather of showing that in an important sense there is no subject; for it alone could *not* be mentioned in the book.—
>
> The subject does not belong to the world; rather, it is a limit of the world.
> Where *in* the world is a metaphysical subject to be found?
> You will say that this is exactly like the case of the eye and the visual field. But really you do *not* see the eye.
> And nothing *in the visual field* allows you to infer that it is seen by an eye . . .
>
> The philosophical self is not the human being, not the human body, or the human soul, with which psychology deals, but rather the metaphysical subject, the limit of the world—not a part of it.[15]

I am not going to try to assess these three philosophical approaches to the notion of the self or subject. But I do think they provide useful devices for making sense of different poets' bodies of work, since the conception of the self that informs the work of a particular poet usually has stronger affinities with one among these three traditional views than with the others. The most familiar conception of the self is that of the Cartesian ego: it is this conception that, I think, grounds any poetry introspective to a significant extent and characterized by a distinctive sense of personality or voice. While there is usually a degree of alienation of the self from the world, that self is still seen as *part* of the world, a part to which the poet has a privileged means of introspective access, and a part whose experiences and nature the poetry ventures to depict (even though the expression may involve a variety of voices and personae—e.g., Berryman's Henry).

The conception of the self underlying Ashbery's poetry is, I believe, that of the transcendental or metaphysical subject; and I think this helps account for the radical difference between his poetry and most other poets for whom the self is a main theme, including ones who have managed to capture some of his characteristic tone and voice. I have already noted some of the reasons for this way of looking at his work: the extreme referential, temporal, and spatial dislocations and transitions in his poems, which make it impossible to read them as an autobiographical record of the experiences of a time-bound, self-identical Cartesian ego; his subject's characteristic impulse to identify or produce an adequate representation of itself while simultaneously distancing itself from every such image, which all become "other" as soon as they become concrete or clear enough (and in this connection note David Kalstone's observation that "Alive in its present, and determined as a Jack-in-the-Box, that self pops up when any moment of poetic concision threatens to obliterate it");[16] and, most important, the fact that despite these tendencies we are aware, reading his poems, of an undeniable "feeling of existence without the least concept [of it]"[17] (to use Kant's characterization of the transcendental subject), together with the impression that it is from the vantage point of this ineffable existence that his poetry monitors the details of the world, among which are his own personality:

> Each detail was startlingly clear, as though seen through a
>     magnifying glass,
> Or would have been to an ideal observer, namely yourself—
> For only you could watch yourself so patiently from afar
> The way God watches a sinner on the path to redemption,
> Sometimes disappearing into valleys, but always *on the way*.
>                                             ("The Bungalows")[18]

Of course Ashbery's is not the only poetry infused with a conception of the self different from the traditional Cartesian one. Frank O'Hara's is another. In the course of discussing O'Hara's poem "Music," Marjorie Perloff observes that

> the pronoun "I" and its cognates appear ten times in the space of twenty-one lines. Yet, unlike the typical autobiographical poem with its circular structure (present-past-return to present with renewed insight), "Music" does not explore the speaker's past so as to determine what has made him the person he is; it does not, for that matter, "confess" or "reveal" anything about his inner psychic life. The role of the "I" is to respond rather than to confess . . . As in Pasternak's *Safe Conduct,* one of O'Hara's favorite books, the "I" fragments into the surfaces it contemplates. Hence the poet can only tell us what he does . . . how he *responds* to external stimuli . . . and what he *recalls* . . . But he makes no attempt to reflect upon the larger human condition, or to make judgments upon his former self, as Robert Lowell does in the *Life Studies* poems . . . It is a matter of reifying a feeling rather than remembering another person or a particular event; in so doing, that feeling becomes part of the poet's present.[19]

This strongly recalls Hume's statement that "when I enter most intimately into what I call *myself,* I always stumble on some particular perception of other, of heat or cold, light or shade, love or hatred, pain or pleasure. I can never catch *myself* at any time without a perception, and can never observe anything but the perception."[20] Many critics have remarked on the diversity among the poets who constitute what used to be called "the New York School"; and certainly in O'Hara and Ashbery the differences in form, voice, and projected personality alone are enormous. But I think the deeper distinction between them involves a difference between the views of the self their works embody. Neither's poetry offers an autobiographical record of the history of a Cartesian mind; but O'Hara's affinity is with Hume's "no self" view, on which the very notion of a self is delusory, corresponds to no reified perception of passion encountered in experience, and has to be dismantled:

```
        I could not change it into history
and so remember it,
                and I have lost what is always and everywhere
present, the scene of my selves, the occasion of these ruses,
which I myself and singly must now kill
                and save the serpent in their midst.
                                ("In Memory of My Feelings")21
```

The vantage point of O'Hara's voice is always situated in real time, in fact, at the moment of writing. But Ashbery's vantage point is an atemporal one from which even the moment of actual utterance seems remote (here compare Kalstone on Ashbery: "Tense will shift while the poem refers to itself as part of the past,"22 with Perloff on O'Hara: "It is a matter of reifying a feeling . . . in so doing, that feeling becomes part of the poet's present").23 Ashbery's impulse is not so much to dismantle the various emblems with which the self might mistakenly try to identify as to try to see them, from the vantage point of the metaphysical subject, as what they really are, things among other things, and so to transcend them:

> So that now in order to avoid extinction it again became necessary to invoke the idea of oneness, only this time if possible on a higher plane, in order for the similarities in your various lives to cancel each other out and the differences to remain, but under the aegis of singleness, separateness, so that each difference might be taken as the type of all the others and yet remain intrinsically itself, unlike anything in the world. Which brings me to the scene in the little restaurant. You are still there, far above me like the polestar and enclosing me like the dome of the heavens; your singularity has become oneness, that is your various traits and distinguishing works have flattened out into a cloudlike protective covering whose irregularities are all functions of its uniformity, and which constitutes an arbitrary but definitive boundary line between the new informal, almost haphazard way of life that is to be mine permanently and the monolithic sameness of the world that exists to be shut out. For it has been measured once and for all. It would be wrong to look back at it, and luckily we are so constructed that the urge to do so can never waken in us. We are both alive and free.
> ("The System")24

There is a curious and exhilarating sense of liberty in Ashbery's work, quite independent of his penchant for syntactic license (which occasionally serves to strain the more genuine sense of freedom his poems convey). I think it is significant, in this connection, that the idea of the transcendental or metaphysical subject was originally invoked by Kant in an effort to reconcile our awareness of that freedom we conceive ourselves as possessing with the fact that any merely psychological ego or personality must, as an object in the natural world, be constrained by the natural laws that govern this world. Writing of an artwork by Owen Morrel called *Asylum*, which he characterizes as a "private and transcendental experience,"[25] Ashbery quotes with evident sympathy the artist's own description of the piece: "If the room/cell becomes the confines of the light/energy of the mind, the open wall points to the future beyond the self—to no mind or one mind. *Asylum* becomes a gateway to a specific kind of freedom available to those who open the right door."[26]

In the last analysis the conception of the metaphysical subject merely serves to make palpable that "specific kind of freedom," that sense that "We are both alive and free," which is one of Ashbery's poetry's most distinctive characteristics and the one that makes it so valuable.

## NOTES

1. In John Ashbery, *Houseboat Days* (New York: Viking, 1978).

2. Kenneth Koch is said to have once remarked that the paradigmatic Ashbery line would be "It wants to go to bed with us."

3. Ashbery, *Houseboat Days*.

4. David Kalstone, *Five Temperaments* (New York: Oxford University Press, 1977), 195.

5. Ashbery, *Houseboat Days*.

6. In John Ashbery, *The Double Dream of Spring* (New York: Dutton, 1970).

7. Ashbery, *Houseboat Days*.

8. In John Ashbery, *Self-Portrait in a Convex Mirror* (New York: Viking, 1975).

9. In John Ashbery, *Rivers and Mountains* (New York: Holt, Rinehart and Winston, 1965).

10. In John Ashbery, *Three Poems* (New York: Viking, 1972).

11. David Hume, *A Treatise of Human Nature* (1739), bk. 1, pt. 4, sec. 6.

12. Immanuel Kant, *Prolegomena to Any Future Metaphysics* (1783), pt. 3, sec. 46.

13. Immanuel Kant, *Critique of Pure Reason* (1781), A350.

14. Arthur Schopenhauer, *The World as Will and Representation* (1818), bk. 2, sec. 278.

15. Ludwig Wittgenstein, *Tractatus Logico-Philosophicus* (1921; London: Routledge and Kegan Paul, 1961), 5.63–641.

16. Kalstone, *Five Temperaments,* 187.

17. Kant, *Prolegomena,* pt. 3, sec. 46.

18. Ashbery, *The Double Dream of Spring.*

19. Marjorie Perloff, *Frank O'Hara: Poet among Painters* (New York: Braziller, 1977), 135–36.

20. Hume, *Treatise,* bk. 1, pt. 4, sec. 6.

21. In Frank O'Hara, *Collected Poems* (New York: Alfred A. Knopf, 1971).

22. Kalstone, *Five Temperaments,* 195.

23. Perloff, *Frank O'Hara,* 136.

24. Ashbery, *Three Poems.*

25. John Ashbery, "Art" column, *New York* 11, no. 35 (August 28, 1978), 104.

26. Ibid.

# The Subject of Extremity
## (1980)

Something poetry, in the broadest sense, aspires to is an understanding of what it is *like* to be whatever it is we are. This is something we need in order to even begin to understand *what* it is we are. Whatever a self or subject is, each of us certainly "is" one, and our experiences are the experiences "of" one. So poetry ought to be able to help us understand what our kind of subject is.

That literature does bear on the problem of the subject is, of course, a commonplace of postmodern literary theory. Indeed, it is sometimes held that a proper approach to literature—a deconstructive one regarding texts irreferentially—is of a piece with a proper philosophical conception of the subject, a conception that is in turn reinforced by the practice of applying such methods even to literary texts to which they may seem ill suited. Before trying to assess this kind of critical tendency, whether to defend it against competing approaches or to urge its revision, there is a more general question that ought to be addressed first but which seldom is: how can poetry, or literature in general, embody, illuminate, or tell for or against any general philosophical conception of the self at all? The purpose of my remarks is to raise a difficulty about the very idea of poetry's doing this and to sketch a possible answer to it—one that is, at least to my mind, not entirely satisfying.

Three broad philosophical conceptions of the self are the *substantival,* the *relational,* and the *perspectival.* They share the idea that there *are* such things as experiences or, as it can also be put, instantiations of mental states. On the substantival conception these states get instantiated by relatively durable

From *Innovation/Renovation,* Wurzburg/Munich, 1980.

pieces of the world called "selves" or "egos," each experience being a property *of* one and each one capable of instantiating an indefinite number of mental states with its identity intact. This view is associated with common sense, Plato, Descartes, Bishop Butler, and ego psychology.

On the relational conception of the subject, a view found in Hume and a good deal of contemporary literary theory, there are no such things or substances as selves to which experiences belong, though talk *of* them may be true enough for all that. *I, myself, this thing that thinks and has experiences*—these terms are irreferential, and what makes statements containing them true are not the instantiations of mental states by the individual thing whose experiences they report but, rather, particular relationships of continuity constituted by memory, intention, and desire, which partition the field of experience into sequences, "bundles of perception," whose subjective coherence gives rise to the idea of a persisting subject, an idea to which nothing real answers.

The relational conception arises from Hume's observation that the self is not experienced: "when I enter most intimately into what I call *myself,* I always stumble on some particular perception or other . . . [but] I never can catch *myself* at any time."[1]

The third conception is at one with Hume in denying that our idea of the self is one of a persisting object but does not follow the relational view in deriving that idea from relations between experiences. Rather, on the perspectival view our conception of individual "selves" is nothing but a conception of the irreducibly perspectival character of experience itself, an attempt, inevitably inept, to formulate the idea that whatever mental state may be instantiated, what makes it an experience and not a dead event, is that *there is something it is like* "for me" to be in it; and that, however much another experience might resemble this one, there is a dimension along which it could not be anything *like* this one at all. One tries to express this by saying "It's mine" or, like Gerard Manley Hopkins:

> Nothing else in nature comes near this unspeakable stress of pitch, distinctiveness, and selving, this self being of my own.

Nothing explains it or resembles it, except so far as this, that other men to themselves have the same feeling. But this only multiplies the phenomena to be explained so far as they are like and do resemble. But to me there is no resemblance: searching nature I taste *self* at one tankard, that of my own being.[2]

The perspectival view is not a conception of a thing (or of a network of relations between things) *in* nature or the world. Is it a conception of a self at all? One is inclined to say so. But this is only an inclination to advertise that the result "searching nature" is the discovery that some objective episodes are private experiences of the world.

These are sketches of three philosophical accounts of what we are. The question isn't of which one is correct but of how poetry might help assess them. The most general relation between philosophy and literature seems to me to be this: literature—and here poetry especially—can enable us to grasp what our experience would be like *if* certain philosophical theories *were* true and thereby help us decide whether they *are* true (by comparing the character of the imagined experience with our own). But when the theories concern the nature of the self a certain difficulty arises.

The difficulty is that, as far as the character of ordinary experience goes, whatever it would be like to be a subject of one of these kinds is the same as what it would be like to be a subject of any of the other kinds. The experience of a substantival self would be of what it would be like to instantiate the conscious mental states that it does; and, as long as this experience includes (as ordinarily it does) the subjective coherence of memory and desire, this is what it would be like to be a subject both on the relational and perspectival conceptions as well. So, if poetry can embody a conception of the self only by conveying what our experience would be like under that conception, then, if it confines itself to the character of *ordinary* experience, it cannot embody any particular conception of the self at all. As far as everyday experience is concerned, all notions of the self are, to borrow a term from logical empiricism, "observationally equivalent": the character of that experience would be roughly the same whichever kind of one we were. "Happy subjects," one might say, "all seem alike."

But to continue the paraphrase: "Each unhappy subject is unhappy in its own way." The difficulty is that the three philosophical conceptions of the self are, in ordinary circumstances, experientially equivalent. And the answer to it is that these three kinds of selves *dissolve* in different ways. The character of the experience of the subject in *extremity,* in the process of disintegration or evaporation, is different under each conception. The dissolution of the substantival or Cartesian ego consists in an increasing *constriction* of its mental arena, until, failing to instantiate any further mental states, it ceases to exist. And the experience of this dissolution is one of an increasing poverty of consciousness, of an inability to consciously experience whatever mental states it may enjoy, of the reversal of Freud's promise "wo es war, da soll Ich sein."[3]

For the relational subject the condition of extremity is not one of diminution or dissolution (since on this view the self is not a thing, and so there is nothing to be diminished or dissolved) but, rather, of the *disruption* of the particular relations between experiences that invest each one with a sense of continuity with the others collectively filling the role of the (nonexistent) self. The experience of this condition would be one of the deterioration or loosening of the sense of connection, furnished by memory and desire, between past, present, and future, and of an intensely heightened experience of the present, with no discernable sense of relation to its before and after.

On the perspectival conception talk of the self is a misleading but unavoidable way of trying to express the perspectival character of subjective experience, the sense that there is something it is *like* for a mental state to be instantiated that cannot, in principle, be captured in a description of the world from an objective viewpoint, that viewpoint thus remaining necessarily incomplete. The experience of the condition of extremity of the perspectival subject, then, is one of the *dissipation* of this sense of the private character of experience and of a correlative *expansion* of the sense of the possibility of a completely objective version of the world, which would locate "our" thoughts and feelings, inlets of memory, and estuaries of desire unproblematically on a map of the world and still leave no aspect uncharted.

All this is to suggest that it is primarily in rendering the experience of extremity, the experience of the contingency of experience, that poetry joins the philosophical issue of the nature of the self (which helps explain, I think, the marginality of much of the poetry that tries to speak directly to the question of what it is we are). But this is not a matter of any particular *way* of writing: there is, as far as I can see, no such thing as a style, a voice, or even a single poetry of extremity. The strain of the individual's voice as it tries to personify its unconscious, its community, or its history, so characteristic of "confessional" poets like Robert Lowell or John Berryman, is the sound of the substantival subject in peril. The euphoric pitch of the present in Frank O'Hara, the vertiginous music of Proust's narrator's early morning walk in the Bois de Boulogne—these are some ways contingency sounds as it settles into the interstices of the relational soul. The sense of the fragility of the perspectival, the speciousness of its kind of privacy—we feel that in the hallucinatory clarity of Kakfa and Elizabeth Bishop, the dissipation of perspective in Thomas Pynchon's Zone, and the indefinitely accommodating mentality of John Ashbery. Neither the condition nor the poetry of extremity is of any fixed or determinate nature.

But this is as it should be, for neither are we, its subjects.


NOTES

1. David Hume, *A Treatise of Human Nature* (1739), bk. 1, pt. 4, sec. 6.

2. Gerard Manley Hopkins, *Sermons and Devotional Writings* (London: Oxford University Press, 1959), 123.

3. Sigmund Freud, *Gesammelte Werke* XV (Frankfurt: S. Fischer Verlag, 1940), 86.

# On Joan Murray
## *(1987)*

The public record contains very little information about Joan Vincent Murray. She was born in London in 1917, during one of the small attacks that passed for air raids in World War I, and was educated in England, France, Canada, and the United States. She attended W. H. Auden's poetry classes at The New School in New York and died in 1942, at the age of twenty-four, in Saranac, New York, of a heart ailment acquired in childhood. At the time of her death she had published only a few poems, in *Decision* and *Chimera,* two little magazines of the day; and her papers were in disarray, with many of her poems apparently not in final form. They were edited, with a few minor revisions and corrections, by Grant Code, and in 1946 the manuscript was chosen by Auden as his first selection for The Yale Series of Younger Poets.

The reception of her poems was on the whole favorable but restrained, with some criticism of their abstraction and detachment, failings that were attributed to her lack of the familiarity with the full range of human experience and emotion that comes with maturity. Yet in retrospect it is these qualities, in combination with others, that render her work original and of continuing interest. Her style betrays some contemporary influences—of Auden, of course, and perhaps also of Laura Riding—in its classical diction and objectivity, its use of personified abstractions, and its occasionally stilted syntax; yet these are outweighed by her own distinctive mood and concerns. Though her tone is didactic in a pleasant and relaxed way, the focus of her address is, unlike Auden's, almost never

From *Poetry Pilot* (June 1987), the newsletter of the Academy of American Poets. Reprinted by permission.

public but more like an internalized objectification of herself. But her work is never hermetic, and, though it is, like Riding's, intellectualized, it has a compassionate, poignant quality entirely absent from Riding's.

Her principal subjects are night, sleep, and dreams as well as a particularly abstract version of the family romance. Unlike most poets whose obsessions are nocturnal, she does not think of sleep and dreaming as unpossessable paradises of symbolic wish-fulfillment but, rather, as conditions in which waking experience is deconstructed and thereby rejuvenated. The rational surface gives her writing a daylight quality, but it owes its strength to its darker underside. She conceives of experience as a confluence of and withdrawal from such personified forces as Mother, Man, Woman, and Child, resulting in a sense of life as isolated and yet adequate ("All things are cool in themselves and complete").[1] These themes are ambitious ones, and their development in the work she was able to produce is somewhat tentative and incomplete. Even so, enough of her poetry is remarkable in its depth, realization, and the way it transcends its period that it deserves to be better known than it is today.

NOTE

1. "Men and Women Have Meaning Only as Man and Woman," in Joan Murray, *Poems* (New Haven, CN: Yale University Press, 1947).

# A Brief Appreciation
## (1989)

James Schuyler's poems seem to me to be the product of a
relentless *gaze*—one that sees the world in accordance with
Bishop Joseph Butler's eighteenth-century dictum, "Each
thing is what it is, and not another thing." Rendering things as
they actually appear is a fundamental principle of modernism
in both poetry and painting; but Schuyler is the only poet I
know of to have really explored and accepted the conse-
quences of this idea. Unlike some latter-day imagist or objectiv-
ist, his gaze is not limited to the perception of the external
world, though it certainly includes it, and he is surely the
preeminent poet of surfaces, textures, skies, smoke, and sea-
sons. But the world also comprises attitudes, attachments,
moods, and regrets that most prevailing perspectives in poetry
view as retrograde, naive, or self-deceptive (as perhaps they
are), and on that account to be disowned. Schuyler's work
stands in contrast to this "poetics of avoidance": in it, the
commonplace is not transfigured but remains defiantly ordi-
nary; but equally, the grandiose retains its grandeur, the senti-
mental retains its integrity (and thus its power), and death
remains both a fact and a fable. It makes the simplest state-
ment and poses the most unsettling question: "This is what
things are like. How do you like them?" The language is as
clear and unswerving as the gaze itself, and the line breaks are
like blinks, which sometimes dissipate a tear.

---

From *Denver Quarterly* 24, no. 4 (spring 1990). Reprinted by per-
mission.

# Contrary Impulses

## *The Tension between Poetry and Theory*
## *(1990)*

> Mrs. Stevens and I went out for a walk yesterday
> afternoon. We walked to the end of Westerly Terrace,
> and she turned left and I turned right.
> —Wallace Stevens[1]

A striking fact of our current literary culture is the estrange-
ment between poets and critics and reviewers of contemporary
poetry, on the one hand, and proponents of that loosely de-
fined set of doctrines, methodologies, and interests that goes by
the name of "theory," on the other. There are individual excep-
tions to this on both sides, and one can find counterexamples to
every generalization I shall suggest here. Nevertheless, anyone
familiar with the climates of opinion to be found in English and
philosophy departments, poetry workshops and critical sympo-
sia, creative writing and cultural studies programs, and the
(dwindling) nonacademic counterparts of these, especially
among people in their twenties and thirties, has to acknowl-
edge the lack of acquaintance and interest—and often even the
disdain and contempt—that characterizes the relations be-
tween poets and those engaged in the kind of high-level, quasi-
philosophical reflective activity that literature, and poetry in
particular, used to occasion. Illustrations are easy to come by.
References to modern poetry by younger theorists are typically
confined to the high modernists and to poets canonized twenty
or thirty years ago in books like Donald Allen's *New American
Poetry* or Richard Howard's *Alone with America;* and their rare

From *Critical Inquiry* 18, no. 1 (fall 1991). Copyright © 1991 by the
University of Chicago. All rights reserved. I am grateful to Herbert
Blau for helpful conversations on the subjects of this essay.

allusions to the poetry of their contemporaries often betray a striking lack of familiarity and taste. Conversely, the fact that, eighty years after Pound called for the breaking of everything breakable, a poet as intelligent and conceptually ambitious as Jorie Graham should title a book *The End of Beauty,* and have the theoretical outlook evoked by the title hailed as radical by as informed a critic as Helen Vendler, surely suggests that the level of reflective awareness in the poetry community is not what it might be.[2]

This estrangement is a recent phenomena. *Theory* currently has a fairly specific sense—or, rather, a number of senses—but in its broadest sense it refers to the kind of reflective activity that aims to articulate and criticize the general principles and assumptions underlying artifacts, practices, and forms of expression taken to have cultural (and, in particular, aesthetic) significance. Theory in this sense was an integral part of the development of modernist poetry, with Eliot's essays, for example, constituting a critique of the enervated poetry of turn-of-the-century England and the culture against which modernist work was to be read; a revision of the canon of Western literature; and an argument for certain principles regarding objectivity, expression, feeling, and knowledge in poetry. And following the establishment of modernism, New Criticism, taken as a whole, provided a sustained theoretical legitimation of the preeminent place poetry had come to occupy in literary culture, in part by endowing it with a distinctive epistemological status as a source of "presentational" (as opposed to "discursive") knowledge of human experience. (New Criticism's insistence on poetry's "fidelity to its own nature" tends to obscure this;[3] but the real point was that poetry's epistemological status is unique to it, rather than the result of features it shares with psychology, history, or science.) Given then that poetry and theoretical reflection, at least in some forms, are not inherently inimical to each other, how might their recent estrangement be explained?

I think it is useful to distinguish here between what might be called "institutional" and "intrinsic" explanations. The former emphasize differences between the cultural and academic settings in which poetry and theory are practiced, while the latter try to identify conceptual tensions between poetry and theory themselves. The distinction is too simple—for surely the ways in which poetry and theory are institutionalized reflect some of their underlying principles, and their institutional settings influence how those principles get articulated and developed—but at least it helps identify the kinds of tensions I want to explore. My interest is in intrinsic or inherent tensions between poetry and theory in their current forms; but I want to look briefly at some of the institutional factors at work (for these may be, in the end, the more important). Contemporary theory, especially in the United States, began as a reaction against New Criticism and has tended ever since to define itself by contrast with the latter's characteristic preoccupations and associations, of which poetry was preeminent. Its rise has also been accompanied by the emergence of cultural and film studies and canon revision as central components of academic literary culture—tendencies that sit uneasily with poetry, whose status as a "high" art form seems difficult to subvert (despite perennial attempts to do so). For its part, the single most striking institutional fact about poetry in the last twenty years has been its incorporation into academic writing programs and workshops, situated (often uneasily) within English departments. Not only has the resultant commodification of poetry tended to preclude (if only for practical reasons) the kind of anxious self-consciousness about writing characteristic of current theory; but also the need for academic legitimation has led most writing programs to require a certain level of familiarity with the kinds of historical and critical texts and outlooks that have been so insistently called into question in literary studies at large.

Theory in its current form comprises a number of disparate doctrines and methodologies, which include deconstruction, critical theory, cultural studies, psychoanalysis, Marxist analysis, feminist criticism, and reception theory. I am going to concentrate on the first of these and try to identify some possible sources of intrinsic tension between poetry and deconstruction. There are several reasons for this limitation. Deconstruction's predecessor, New Criticism, had an intimate conceptual relation to poetry, whereas most of the other current theoretical tendencies had no particular historical association with it. Thus any tensions between deconstruction and poetry are more likely to be intrinsic, and therefore more interesting, than in the cases of the other theoretical tendencies. In addition, deconstruction's obsessions with the possibilities and limitations of the expression of thought and experience, and with the status of the subjective self, are ones it shares with most of the poetry that I think merits being taken seriously.

Deconstruction is not an easy view to characterize. As a philosophical position in the strict sense, as originally formulated by Derrida, I take it to be something like the view that there is nothing either in the circumstances of the employment of tokens of repeatable signs or signifiers, or in the intentions or conscious mental states of language users that fixes their meanings or symbolic contents or associates with them determinate concepts. Rather, they are subject to multiple, shifting interpretations based on past and future instances of employment that are never "present." This philosophical view has interesting similarities to those of such mainstream philosophers of language as W. V. Quine, Donald Davidson, and Wittgenstein (particularly on Saul Kripke's reading of him), though there are significant differences too (especially over the appropriate constraints on interpretation).[4]

Whether or not there are tensions between poetry and deconstruction in its purely philosophical form seems to me a moot question, as it isn't in this form that it usually impinges on literary studies and practice. Moreover, philosophical deconstruction isn't really a body of doctrines or claims at all but an attempt to break the hold of certain illusions about the source or ground of linguistic meaning. It would only be at odds then with conceptions of poetry that essentially subscribed to those illusions; and few do (though what I term below the "instrumental" conception of poetry may be one that does).

Yet philosophical deconstruction is often invoked by those engaged in deconstructive criticism of specifically literary texts; and that critical practice is in turn often taken to illustrate or support certain general claims about language and mentality that may be at some remove from the philosophical original. In *The Linguistic Moment,* for instance, J. Hillis Miller gives a reading of Stevens in which three conceptions of poetry—as depiction, as discovery, and as creation—are simultaneously in play, though the poet's commitment to them is irresolvably indeterminate. The "linguistic moment" at which this indeterminacy emerges exemplifies "the effacement of extra-linguistic reference initiated by the apparent act of self-reference."[5] And this effacement or indeterminacy is said by Miller to be due neither to any pecularity of the literary text, nor the author's confusion, nor to limitations of the reader's interpretative powers; it arises, rather, "as an intrinsic necessity of language," that "airy and spacious prison" in which Western literature has resided for twenty-five hundred years.[6] Thus over and above deconstruction in the strict philosophical sense there is deconstruction as it figures in the discussion of specifically literary texts, as it informs theoretical speculation within literary studies, and as it tends to be perceived by writers and critics of poetry. And it is deconstruction in this form—a debased form, if you will—that I think is important in the present context.

The central claim of this more widely received version of deconstruction is that all forms of linguistic or symbolic representation are marked by radical indeterminacy. The notions that terms possess determinate meanings and references, that assertions have well-defined contents, that statements possess objective truth-conditions, and that texts have uniquely correct interpretations are to be rejected as illusory. Moreover, since there is no such thing as the unmediated expression of thought or feeling, all such expression being mediated by inherently indeterminate symbolic systems or texts, the idea of determinate, prelinguistic cognitive and emotional states, fidelity to whose contents is the criterion of a text's accuracy and authenticity, is illusory as well. More generally, the whole notion of an objectively existing Cartesian self or subject possessing a privileged introspective access to its own thoughts, feelings, and intentions is an illusory one. Nevertheless, these illusions are powerful and pervasive, engendered by systems of interpersonal, social, and political arrangements and institutions that they in turn help justify and maintain. It thus becomes an important task of deconstructive criticism to make this inherent indeterminacy manifest, particularly in the kinds of literary texts whose hallmarks are commonly taken to be genuineness and authenticity.

The merits of the case for this outlook are really beside the point here; what matters is that it is widespread and influential. What I do think is important to recognize is that the *impulse* behind the outlook is, in a certain sense, a philosophical one. This may sound odd, especially in light of the antiphilosophical rhetoric of deconstruction's attack on "logocentrism" and the "Western metaphysics of presence" and its preference for strategies of verbal play over those of rational argumentation. But in suggesting that its fundamental impulse is philosophical, I am alluding to the fact that its basic gesture is one of *unmasking:* the illusory nature of commonly accepted ideas of language and the self is to be made apparent, and the arbitrariness of the assumptions governing expression and interpretation is to be revealed. It thus manifests the impulse with which the pre-Socratics inaugurated Western philosophy, namely, the refusal to acquiesce in what thereby comes to be regarded as the realm of appearance, and which opens the way for the introduction of *some* version of the distinction between appearance and reality. This needs qualification. In saying that deconstruction's impulse is philosophical, I am not claiming that the product of that impulse is a body of philosophical texts. Philosophical texts presuppose criteria of response, assessment, and disagreement; and the strategy of deconstructive writing is usually to distance itself from these sorts of criteria. Also, deconstruction's critique of metaphysics is essentially a rejection of "realist" notions of objectivity and truth and of the foundationalist epistemologies that have traditionally accompanied them; and I am not suggesting that it seeks to introduce different versions of the appearance/reality distinction, or different epistemologies, in their stead. Yet the underlying impulse— the refusal of what, by that very refusal, comes to be seen as appearance—is, I believe, a protophilosophical one. The fact that this movement of unmasking is to be continued indefinitely, with the removal of each mask revealing a further one, should not be allowed to obscure the fundamental character of the gesture.

Now I think that much of the intrinsic tension between deconstructive theory and poetry is due to the fact that a contrary impulse is at work in poetry. But before turning to this, I want to note a much more obvious incompatibility between deconstruction and one familiar conception of poetry, a conception that might be called the "instrumental" one. According to this conception, poems are instruments or vehicles for the public expression of something conceptually independent of and prior to themselves—actual or imaginary historical or personal events, individual experiences, or states of perception, thought, and feeling. Successful poems create a sense of authenticity or fidelity to this "prepoetic given" and convey its character in a manner that is vivid, engaging, clear, or affecting. And just as poems themselves are mere instruments for achieving these ends, so the rhetorical and semantic possibilities of language are themselves only instruments for helping them achieve them.

It is obvious that this conception of poetry is at odds with deconstruction's emphasis on the radical indeterminacy of thought and expression, and on the illusory nature of the notions of the prelinguistic given and the subjective self. Yet one may wonder how widespread this conception of poetry actually is. Shouldn't it have been a casualty of New Criticism's insistence on a poem's organic unity and unparaphrasability and confined by now to examples of the primitively confessional sorts of poems Randall Jarrell likened to severed limbs? But I think its influence is more pervasive than this description of it may suggest. To take a random example that comes to hand, in a recent symposium on kitsch Charles Molesworth adduced Rupert Brooke's "The Soldier" as an example of the genre.[7] While there was disagreement among the participants as to whether the poem actually fell under that concept, there was virtual unanimity in the judgment that it was a "bad poem," for the reasons summarized by Irving Howe: its "overblown language" is "inflated, false, stale, etc."[8] Yet the poem is not without interest. Instead of emphasizing the "overblown" and "false" character of the language, one could as well note the pleasurable ease with which the perspective of the poem's subject moves from the personal to the transcendental. True, the movement is not an unfamiliar one, however deftly accomplished, and the poem's failure to acknowledge this is a limitation. But I think it is symptomatic of the appeal of the instrumental conception of poetry that the symposium participants' shared perception of the poem was not one of limitation but of falsehood and a failure of authenticity.

Now as I hope to make clear in a moment, I am not simply identifying this conception of poetry—which obviously I regard as a retrograde one—with the adoption of the rhetorical strategy of truthfulness. In fact, my main complaint about current theoretical perspectives on poetry is that they tend to regard the fact that a certain poetic mode or stance is a linguistic or social construction (rather than something natural or inevitable) as a reason to disown it. My point is that the prevalence of the identification of "good poems" with truthful ones indicates the widespread acceptance of an idea of poetry that presupposes, to adapt Wittgenstein's phrase, "a criterion which gives us a conception of [poetic] 'truth' as distinct from 'truthfulness.' "[9]

The institutionalization of poetry in writing programs has, in an indirect way, helped reinforce the instrumental conception. This is not because, as is often claimed, writing programs instill a formulaic approach to the writing of verse. Just the opposite is more likely to be the case. Most writing programs are free—too free—of any sort of theoretical orientation that sanctions some forms of writing and excludes others. The fact is that it is institutionalizations of poetry that include a large theoretical component that tend to be exclusionary—the Black Mountain and St. Mark's schools come to mind and, more recently, the Language poets. Writing programs are not usually "schools" in this sense. But this tolerance is not, to my mind, a virtue. In the absence of explicitly articulated theoretical principles regarding the nature and purpose of poetry, they inculcate, by default, a poetics of the "individual voice" that valorizes authenticity and fidelity to its origins in prepoetic experience or emotion. The avoidance of any overt theoretical orientation thus reinforces, in the institutionalized setting of the writing program, the particular theoretical conception of poetry I have been calling the instrumental one.

Yet I think there is a deeper source of tension between deconstructive theory and poetic practice that is independent of this conception of poetry. By way of approaching it, I want to remark briefly on the most conspicuous exception to the current estrangement between poetry and theory, the school of Language writers. These poets share with deconstructionists a rejection of the idea that poetic language provides a natural, transparent medium for the transmission of a psychological content or meaning that is constituted independently of its expression; and much of their theoretical writings constitute a sustained polemic against the forms of poetry they take to embody it. To this extent, their influence is salutary (though their characterization of the tainted forms as "officially sanctioned verse"—which usually seems to include everything other than Language poetry—is not particularly illuminating). Against this naturalistic idea of language and content, they argue that our ordinary notions of meaning, which we take to be inevitable, are really social constructions constituted by contingent conventions. The most important aim of poetry is to make this manifest, both by deploying words in ways that focus attention on them and dispel the aura of transparency with which poems usually invest them and by disrupting the conventions that shape our ordinary expectations in reading poems. This requires the scrupulous avoidance of the rhetorical strategies they associate with what they think of as conventional poetry, including the use of the first person (with its implications of reportage and communication), narrative voice (with its suggestions of causal and temporal coherence), and the heightening of affect at closure.

This is an awfully restrictive and didactic view of the function of poetry. The important point, though, is that none of it really follows from the premise that meaning, including meaning in poetry, is socially constructed via conventions of which we are not usually aware. The fact that what we call "the expression of feeling," for example, is a social construction resting on contingent practices and conventions, rather than a natural concomitant of human nature, does not imply that there isn't any such thing or that its practice is the result of an arbitrary decision that we might just as well refuse to make. This is related to my earlier reservation about identifying the instrumental conception of poetry with the rhetorical quality of truthfulness. The use of certain rhetorical modes may signal a commitment to a particular theoretical view of language and meaning, but it is never equivalent to it. Rejecting naturalistic conceptions of expression and Cartesian accounts of the self in favor of views that argue for the social constitution of these notions may involve a reorientation of one's attitude towards them but should not prevent one from exploring and exploiting all the expressive possibilities afforded by language, however socially constituted these may be. Just *how* this reorientation might be made manifest is another question, and a difficult one. But the important thing to see—a point that Stanley Cavell has stressed repeatedly and on which he parts company with deconstruction—is that locating the source of our notions of language, thought, and the mind in contingent human practices does not automatically render them illusory.[10]

I think that a deep source of tension between theory and poetry, at least as I conceive it, lies in a difference in their attitudes towards the fact of the contingent basis of human communicative practices. I realize of course that my conception of poetry isn't universally shared and that other conceptions would locate the source of tension differently or even deny it altogether. Still, I hesitate to think of this account of the resistance of poetry to theory as an entirely personal one, since it seems to me to be related to tensions that pervade thought and expreience generally, regardless of the particular poetics to which one might happen to subscribe. I tend to share Harold Bloom's view that the context in which poetry has to locate itself—and this includes high modernism as well as its contemporary descendants—is one essentially grounded in romanticism. Romanticism's characteristic impulse, to put it very generally, is subjectivity's contestation of its objective situation, which is ultimately one of anonymity or soullessness or nonexistence and death. The tension is grounded in the conviction—which

Thomas Nagel has articulated quite forcefully—that many of the most important aspects of experience can only be apprehended from a "subjective" viewpoint, that they cannot be reduced to or rendered in factual or objective terms, are in some sense not communicable in language, and indeed in some sense are not factually real at all.[11] And by the impulse of contestation I mean the impulse to appropriate (or, perhaps more accurately, misappropriate) language and other forms of communication either in a misconceived attempt to reify these aspects of experience or (more poignantly) to try to demonstrate the limitations of an entirely objective view of the world. And I take this impulse to be characteristic of romanticism in some very broad sense.

Now the particular form this impulse is going to take depends on how the objective situation is perceived. This is complicated for us (as it has been for some time) by the fact that this setting not only includes the literary heritage of romanticism itself but also, I would argue, a theoretical component constituted in large part by modernist and deconstructive readings of the texts that make up that heritage. Thus our version of the romantic impulse of contestation seems almost bound to have the self-reflexive, oedipal character Bloom describes, marked by an intense awareness both of the natural and temporal situation against which it is directed and of that setting's historical, social, and textual constitution; and marked also by a certain blindness, or at least indifference, towards its own participation in that situation.

I would not want to call this context in which poetry is located a "postromantic" one, for that would imply that there was at one time an unselfconscious attitude called "romanticism" that has now been superseded; and the point about the romantic impulse of subjectivity's contestation of its objective setting is that the form it takes alters as the perception of that setting is altered by the awareness of its historical and textual antecedents. Perhaps it is too essentialistic to say that poetry *has to* locate itself in this context. But it does seem to me that for poetry to remove itself from it entirely is for it to abandon the realm of enactment for the realm of illustration, as in the case of the instrumental poetry of the authentic voice, which I think merely exemplifies an untenable conception of thought and expression; and, in the case of Language poetry, which is too content to merely illustrate the ways in which meaning is conventionally constructed.

Now the contestation that poetry enacts is almost bound to embody such characteristic movements as desire, expansiveness, regret, disappointment, despondency, consolation, and resignation; for it is in terms like these that subjectivity defines itself against its objective setting. The ways in which these movements manifest themselves within the poetic field of the imagination are never (one would hope) straightforward and ingenuous; yet it is difficult to envisage a poetic imagination from which they are entirely absent. Moreover, these movements are realized in poems by rhetorical devices and strategies that are, let us grant, textual and social constructions; and poems that fail to acknowledge this, and which deploy them in a completely unselfconscious manner, enact at best a limited and weak version of romantic contestation (recall the Brooke poem). Yet despite all this, contestation is an active and assertoric gesture (even when its major movements are ones like resignation and regret); and this requires, at *some* level of theoretical self-awareness, a kind of *acquiescence* in the affective movements by which it is constituted and the rhetorical conventions by which these movements are realized.

Earlier I suggested that the impulse behind deconstruction is the protophilosophical one of unmasking, an impulse that attempts to demonstrate that interpretations and forms of expression that would ordinarily be regarded as natural are actually the products of contingent human conventions and practices, that alternatives to them are conceivable, and that therefore (*sic*) attributions of thought and meaning are to be consigned to the realm of appearance. Its basic gesture is one of *refusal*, since it insists on disassociating itself from any conventions and practices—and from the units of significance they help create—which it is not, in some sense, "logically compelled" to accept. But this gesture is in sharp contrast to the one produced by the impulse of romantic contestation that I believe to be central to poetry; for that impulse requires (again, at *some* level) an acquiescence in the affective

movements and rhetorical strategies by which it is enacted—
that is to say, an acquiescence in what, from the vantage point
of deconstruction, amounts to mere appearance. It isn't that
the romantic impulse is entirely incompatible with the sort
of theoretical awareness that gives rise to deconstruction—
indeed, that awareness ought to be expected to help shape
the perception of the objective situation against which the
impulse is directed. It is, rather, that deconstruction holds
(wrongly, in my view) that this awareness dictates an attitude
towards human communicative practices generally and poetic
practice in particular that is at odds with the stance towards
language and expression poetic practice demands. This isn't
to say that deconstructionist views of language and thought
are somehow "mistaken"; and I think it is important to ac-
knowledge that the poetic impulse I have been trying to char-
acterize involves a considerable degree of theoretical bad
faith—not the gratuitous kind of bad faith exemplified by the
poetry of authenticity but, rather, the ineliminable kind mani-
fested in, say, Wittgenstein's writing the *Tractatus* in the full
certainty of his belief in its unintelligibility or by the defiant
assurance that "I sing alway" with which John Ashbery con-
cludes "Fantasia on 'The Nut-Brown Maid.' "[12]

It may seem odd to assimilate deconstructive theory to the
impulse towards the refusal of appearance that is characteris-
tic of philosophical realism; yet I think that this assimilation
not only helps locate a fundamental source of tension between
poetry and that theoretical perspective but also provides some
sense of what a poetics informed by theoretical reflection in a
broader sense might be like. Such a poetics would neither
reject the domain of subjectivity, as deconstruction does, nor
try to incorporate it into the domain of the objective, as the
poetics of authenticity tries to do. Unfortunately, this kind of
poetics remains largely unformulated, and, given the institu-
tional factors I described earlier, I am not terribly optimistic
about its prospects. One conspicuous exception to this bleak
outlook is furnished by Allen Grossman's writings, whose
"speculative poetics" make up a sustained body of thought
about the nature and possibilities of poetry informed by theo-
retical reflection of a very high order.[13] He takes the function

of poetry to be the preservation of the image of a person against the eroding forces of society and time. But he also insists on distinguishing what he means by a "person" from the familiar psychological notion of the self—the subject of social relationships, autobiography, and the kind of poetry that would ordinarily be called personal or confessional. "Preserving the image of a person" seems to come to something like enacting the demands of subjectivity, of demonstrating that there is something that it is actually *like* to be alive, against the eradicating forces of the impersonal and the real. I think that it is significant that the presiding philosophical figure in Grossman's poetics is Emmanuel Levinas (rather than Derrida), for whom the human face stands not only as a nonrepresentational (and nondeconstructible) emblem of alterity or radical metaphysical otherness but also as a moral injunction not to kill, or as the demand for the preservation of something literally inconceivable. For I think that if poetry is going to recover our attention and respect, it has to reconceive itself as the mind's acknowledgment of this injunction and begin to see itself as one effort among others to maintain the demands of subjectivity and the imagination against the inexorable encroachments of the real.

## NOTES

1. Quoted in Peter Brazeau, *Parts of a World: Wallace Stevens Remembered—An Oral Biography* (New York: Random House, 1983), 43.

2. Helen Vendler, "Married to Hurry and Grim Song," *New Yorker,* July 27, 1987.

3. Rene Wellek and Austin Warren, *Theory of Literature,* 3d ed. (New York: Harcourt Brace Jovanovich, 1977), 37.

4. For a reading of Derrida's arguments in *Limited Inc* along these lines, together with an interesting comparison of his views with those of philosophers like W. V. Quine and Donald Davidson, see Samuel T. Wheeler III, "Indeterminacy of French Interpretation: Derrida and Davidson," in *Truth and Interpretation: Perspectives on the Philosophy of Donald Davidson,* ed. Ernest LePore (Oxford: Oxford University Press, 1986), 477–94.

5. J. Hillis Miller, *The Linguistic Moment* (Princeton: Princeton University Press, 1985), 4.

6. Miller, *Linguistic Moment*, 45, 55.

7. "On Kitsch: A Symposium," *Salmagundi* 85–86 (Winter–Spring 1990): 279.

8. "On Kitsch," 282, 306.

9. Ludwig Wittgenstein, *Philosophical Investigations*, 3d ed., trans. G. E. M. Anscombe (New York: Macmillan, 1968), 223.

10. For a useful exposition of Cavell's views, especially regarding their relation to literature and deconstruction, see Michael Fischer, *Stanley Cavell and Literary Skepticism* (Chicago: University of Chicago Press, 1989).

11. See Thomas Nagel, *The View from Nowhere* (Oxford: Oxford University Press, 1986).

12. John Ashbery, "Fantasia on 'The Nut-Brown Maid,' " *Houseboat Days* (New York: Viking, 1977).

13. See Allen Grossman, "Summa Lyrica: A Primer of the Commonplaces in Speculative Poetics," *Western Humanities Review* 44 (Spring 1990): 5–138; and *Against Our Vanishing* (Boston: Rowan Tree Press, 1981), 14–15.

# The Absence of a Noble Presence
## *(1990)*

> Perhaps you are being kept here
> Only so that somewhere else the peculiar light of someone's
> Purpose can blaze unexpectedly in the acute
> Angles of the rooms.
> —John Ashbery, "Clepsydra"

The character of John Ashbery's influence on contemporary poetry has been shaped in large part by how his own reputation has developed. He is acknowledged to be one of the most significant living American poets and one of the genuinely important poets of this century, a consensus that has formed dramatically during the last fifteen years. Yet a passion for his work by a limited, and largely nonacademic, audience—and the influence of his work on a small number of poets—goes back at least twenty years beyond that. It isn't easy to remember, from the accommodating, directionless, and rather passionless perspective of poetry today, that his poetry originated at a time when there really *was* an important distinction to be drawn—and felt—between the Academy and its Other and that for the most part his work was belittled or ignored by the former and championed all the more fervently for that fact by the latter. One private example: I recall writing an enthusiastic—and, I thought at the time, quite densely argued—review in the campus newspaper of a reading he gave at Princeton in 1966, only to learn that it was regarded with amusement by some of the faculty in the English department as symptomatic of the naïveté of the student literati who'd organized the event.

From *The Tribe of John: Ashbery and Contemporary Poetry,* ed. Susan Schultz (Tuscaloosa: University of Alabama Press, 1995). Reprinted by permission.

The acceptance of his work by the poetry reading public—such as it is—only began, I think, with Harold Bloom's recognition of the importance of *The Double Dream of Spring* in the early 1970s and was only established in 1976 by the accolades accorded *Self-Portrait in a Convex Mirror.*

I've rehearsed the history of the reception of Ashbery's own work because I think it bears on the question of the nature of its influence, an influence that strikes me as somewhat problematic. Part of it is diffuse and reflected in its role in the remodeling of what might be thought of as the "generic" poem of the age from what it amounted to thirty years ago. Part of it is the direct effect it has had on the development—but often, alas, the lack of development—of particular poets and schools of poetry. Yet it seems to me that, with a couple of exceptions, neither its diffuse nor direct influence really reflects or responds to the distinctive aspects of his work that occasioned them in the first place.

My own sense of how other poets have responded to Ashbery's work, and of the respects in which that response has seemed wanting, has been shaped by my own involvement with it; and I want to try to describe some of the perceived characteristics of his poetry that originally drew me to it so strongly, since I have the impression that many of these perceptions are not widely shared. When I started writing seriously in the early 1960s, the poems that helped form, from a distance, my conception of what poetry could and ought to be were principally the high modernist works of Yeats, Eliot, Pound, and Williams—the latter three especially, and especially in the linguistically fragmented modes of "The Waste Land," *The Cantos,* and *Pictures from Brueghel* (along with, from an even greater distance, the poems of Keats, Shelley, and Tennyson). The contemporary models I tried to emulate were the Black Mountain poets Charles Olson, Robert Creely, and Robert Duncan, whose writings seemed to me to combine the ambition and seriousness of the high moderns with a compelling theoretical argument for the centrality of language to perception and thought. Duncan's work in particular became my first real poetic obsession, for the way it managed to incorporate a Shelleyian lyricism and romanticism into the austere and discontinuous linguistic framework of projective verse. In all these poets' works I found a scale of ambition, a conceptual purpose, a concern for the nature and possibilities of the medium of poetry, and a powerful affective element that made the work of more academically acclaimed poets like Robert Lowell, Theodore Roethke, and Richard Wilbur seem tidy and smug by comparison and that of Beat poets like Allen Ginsberg and Lawrence Ferlinghetti emotionally conventional and unselfconscious in its exploitation of rhetoric.

When, against this background, I came across a copy of *The Tennis Court Oath* in 1965, it completely changed my conception of what poetry could be and in a real sense changed my life (for it showed that the relation between poetry and one's life could be much more direct than I'd ever imagined). Here were poems whose linguistic disruptions and conceptual disorientations were far more extreme than anything I'd ever encountered; yet, rather than falling apart or simply becoming inert, they seemed permeated by a romantic sensibility purer and more intense than anything I'd experienced in Duncan's work. I know that this is a somewhat idiosyncratic reading of *The Tennis Court Oath,* but I still think of it as an essentially *lyric* book, a powerful expression of philosophical dualism in which the body and indeed "all that is solid melts into air,"[1] until only a dispersed and decentered subjectivity remains. And, possibly because I came to this book just shortly before the publication of *Rivers and Mountains,* I felt a greater sense of continuity between the radically polarized linguistic constructions of the former and the dense, meditative ruminations inaugurated by the seminal poem "Clepsydra" in the latter than many other readers seemed to perceive. True, the conventions of syntax were largely restored, and the poems adopted a tone of logical or narrative progression. Yet the landscape these restorations helped reconstruct wasn't a tangible setting in the external world at all but, rather, an abstract "region that is no place."[2] And the kind of consciousness arrayed against it—and arrayed, it seemed to me, so furiously—wasn't the familiar subject of the speaking voice but a diffuse, impersonal, and transcendent subjectivity.

I said earlier that I think that the influence of Ashbery's

work takes roughly two forms: first, a broad influence on the character of the kind of poem the literary culture regards as stereotypical and that young poets in their formative stages— at least young poets without prior theoretical allegiances—try (or get accused of trying) to emulate; and, second, its direct influence on particular poets and schools of poetry.

The first of these is largely a product of the celebrity his work has achieved since the mid-1970s, a period in which he has displaced Robert Lowell as the paradigmatic poetic figure of the day (although I know that similar claims can be made for James Merrill in this regard). The exemplary poem of thirty years ago was characterized by a strong speaking voice, and the criteria of its success were the authenticity of that voice and the force and clarity with which the states of feeling, thought, and perception of the person from whom it originated were conveyed. The relation of the poet to the poem was one of *control* (even when the emotions the poem incorporated were passive), and its style was marked by literalness, a clipped diction, an avoidance of indeterminacy, an insistence on the concrete and the particular, and the calculated refusal of rhetorical effect. It rarely acknowledged its status as writing, and its attitude towards the impulses of romanticism was one of irony and condescension.

The generic poem of today seems quite different (though just as unappealing and, fortunately, just as nonexistent). The tone is liable to be nostalgic and its motions those of reverie. Its predominant feelings are passive ones like resignation and loss; its language is resonant and suggestive; the use of the narrative past tense invests it with a mythological quality; and its overall effect is one of tenderness. It dissociates itself, especially in its transitions and patterns of inference, from everyday ideas of rationality and control; its awareness of language is informed by a sense of its limitations; and it is likely to incorporate an apology for its status as writing and for the processes of the imagination that produced it.

This poem is constituted in large part by qualities that have been associated with Ashbery's work since its public reception in the 1970s—passivity, an acquiescence in indeterminacy, an avoidance of rationality, and self-reflexivity. Of course other poets have contributed to its constitution as well—W. S. Merwin, Mark Strand, and James Wright come to mind, and there are several others. But what strikes me as problematic about this aspect of Ashbery's influence is its superficiality. The current generic poem is usually deployed as a stylistic variation on the underlying conception of poetry exemplified by its earlier incarnation: that poetry ought to be a vehicle for the expression, formulation, and validation of a self-conception or personality, or of states of mind. Of course the personality and states of mind it is called on to validate today aren't those of thirty years ago, a difference that is reflected in the nature of the poetry that is supposed to accomplish the task. But then clothes, manners, and attitudes aren't what they were thirty years ago either. Yet one thing that can never be said of Ashbery's poetry is that its primary function is to serve as a vehicle of personal self-expression. This is not to say that it lacks a distinctive psychological character—indeed, the most problematic aspect of its influence is a misapprehension of what its psychological (or, better, spiritual) character actually is. But, to the extent that it has merely furnished a poetic vehicle or style that can be deployed in the service of a conception of poetry that is antithetical to it, its influence has been disappointing.

Ashbery's direct influence on certain schools of poetry has been more interesting but here, too, not as fruitful as it might be. This influence developed prior to, or at least independent of, the public vogue for his work and can be seen, I think, in two broad groups of writers: the first might be called the second (or I suppose by now, the $n$th) generation New York school poets, while the second comprises poets of a more theoretical orientation, currently typified by the Language poets. The strain in Ashbery's work to which the New York school poets seem most responsive is a domestic and deflationary one: the texture of daily life and the experience of ordinary pleasures, perplexities, and disappointments come to replace, or to be placed on a level with, movements like loss, disillusionment, the passage of time, and death as catalysts for the poetic imagination. At the same time, the imagination itself gets reconceived not in terms of transcendence but as a method for recovering the immanence of the everyday. This tendency sometimes issues in a knowing and patronizing antiaestheticism, but at its best it is capable of yielding poems of a refreshing, casual lyricism, reflective of certain moments that are actually present in Ashbery's own work.

The more theoretically inclined poets who have responded to Ashbery's work tend to limit their enthusiasm to *The Tennis Court Oath* and *Three Poems,* often showing little interest in his later books and viewing Bloom's assimilation of his work to the main line of American poetry running through Whitman and Stevens less as a vindication of it than as an act of academic co-optation. Their interest is in the deconstructive aspects of his writing, in which a refusal to conform to or acknowledge poetic conventions and expectations leads to an awareness of their essential arbitrariness and a heightened sense of the palpability of language itself. The main impulse is neither expressive nor lyric but philosophical: to argue that the ordinary conception of language as a natural, transparent medium for the communication of prelinguistic feelings and thoughts is a socially constructed one, maintained in part by the aura of linguistic directness with which poetry is commonly endowed.

While there are poets in both of these schools who have produced individual poems of great accomplishment and interest, I must admit that I find Ashbery's influence somewhat disappointing on the whole. Though there are exceptions (and I want to turn to this shortly), what seem lacking are substantial bodies of work by individual poets that manifest his influence but have a distinctive character of their own. This isn't the case with other poets of something like Ashbery's stature—with James Merrill, for instance, one can cite examples like Alfred Corn, Richard Kenny, and J. D. McClatchy of poets whose works have been partially shaped by his but which still manage to exhibit characteristic obsessions and directions of their own. In some ways Ashbery's case resembles Eliot's, another poet of enormous reputation and importance, whose work was a dominant influence on the generic poem of its day but for whom it is difficult to identify major figures whose works constitute his legacy (though I would argue that in some respects Ashbery himself is such a figure).

Why is this? In what strikes me as an extremely insightful

remark, Allen Grossman has observed about Ashbery's poetry that

> it is the sentimentality of his relationship to the past that he seeks to conserve in a structure which has, as he says, the shape, or anti-shape, of falling snow, but which is still a world characterized by snow and by rain and by sentiment: it is still a landscape with the seeds of tragedy inside it, seeds which he does not allow to germinate, but from the promise of which he derives his significance as a writer. Ashbery . . . is fundamentally a manager of traditional resources.[3]

I think that this is correct. And the traditional resources he seeks to conserve are the fundamental impulses of romanticism, which I would characterize as subjectivity's contestation of its objective setting in a world that has no place for it and which threatens to reduce it to nonexistence. (I also think that much the same can be said of Eliot, though we have only lately begun to read him this way.) But the form that the romantic contestation takes in Ashbery's work is a belated one, differing from its traditional manifestations in several respects. For one thing, it does not attempt to valorize the individual self but, rather, to assert the claims of the diffuse, impersonal subjectivity I spoke of earlier. Moreover, it is informed throughout by an acknowledgment of its own failure ("I am only a transparent diagram, of manners and / Private words with the certainty of being about to fall"),[4] an awareness that accounts for the passivity that is often wrongly taken to be the central emotional tendency in his work—wrongly, because in Ashbery the contestation isn't less intense for being futile ("But its fierceness was still acquiescence / To the nature of this goodness already past").[5] Traditionally the self seeks to reestablish its claims in the face of the magnitude of the natural, objective world through the Kantian experience of the sublime. And it is a mark of our distance from even as recent a formulation of that response as "The Auroras of Autumn" that the possibility of such a resolution is altogether absent from Ashbery's poetry.

Now, while the romantic impulse underlying Ashbery's work has been noted by critics like Bloom, it seems to me that the poets most directly influenced by his poetry have not, for the most part, responded to that impulse very strongly. There are of course instances of Ashbery's style being adopted in the service of the poetic enterprise of the validation of the individual self, a stereotypically romantic one—but this is quite different from the abstract version of romantic contestation his poetry enacts. The poets who have been most directly influenced by his work, and whose interest in it largely predates its more public acceptance, have tended to emphasize either its domestic and deflationary aspects or else its deconstructive ones. I consider this unfortunate. These aspects are genuine, but I think of them as merely part of the form the diffuse, decentered version of romantic contestation takes in his poetry, almost as though this whole glittering postmodern contraption were powered by an old-fashioned wood-burning stove.

I think these generalizations about the ways poets have responded to Ashbery's work are roughly correct; but there are important exceptions to them. Of the poets whose writing is marked by Ashbery's influence yet which has an integrity and substance of its own, the most fully realized is Douglas Crase in *The Revisionist*. He takes over the high meditative style that emerges in Ashbery from "Clepsydra" on: long, fluent lines that unroll in supple movements through unbroken and extended verse paragraphs; a tone of argument that remains poised and abstract even though couched in terms that are mostly casual and colloquial; and an emotional undercurrent that gathers slowly but insistently and with great culminative force. Yet his poetry also enacts a distinctive and original version of the romantic contestation central to Ashbery's.

Crase is a more public poet than Ashbery, not so much in terms of his poetry's intended audience as in the ways in which its subjectivity and its objective setting are conceived. In Ashbery the objective setting is a fragmented personal world constituted by an inaccessible past, disrupted relationships, and communicative indeterminacy; and the subjectivity is an almost solipsistic one. The objective setting of Crase's poetry is a geographic America in which anonymity and collective forgetfulness have become the conditions of mere being, against which he deploys an Emersonian transcendental consciousness that tries to establish itself by reimagining that setting, an act in which the pathetic fallacy gets raised nearly to the power of truth.

One way of characterizing the difference between Ashbery's and Crase's work—one that also helps clarify the sense in which Ashbery's is "private" while Crase's is "public"—is in terms of the structure of the subjective consciousness that informs each of them. Both are enactments of the process whereby the raw materials of an archaic, primary mentality get transformed into conceptualized thought through the activities of interpretation and acknowledgment, a fragile and never completed process constantly threatened by the possibilities of failure and regression.[6] In Ashbery's work this process is closer to the original Freudian paradigm, with the archaic, primary material being something like the hallucinated objects of wish-fulfillment, constantly on the verge of coalescing into a rational narrative structure that always dissolves just as it is about to be achieved. In Crase, though, the primary raw material, which simply presents itself without explanation, isn't the private phantasmagoria of the hallucination or dream but the common locales and features of the contemporary American landscape, which for us have regressed into a kind of immediate meaninglessness. His poetry enacts the effort to transform (or restore) this material to significance though a process of identification, acceptance, and love—a process that, if successfully completed, would result not in the mature rationality towards which Ashbery's poetry gestures but, rather, in a transcendental vantage point that views our common setting, *sub specise aeternatitis,* from an almost planetary perspective. As with Ashbery, what the poetry presents is the process itself, rather than the completed conceptualization towards which it points (though oddly enough Crase's work seems somewhat more optimistic about the possibility of achieving its aims than Ashbery's, even though its aims are more grandiose). And also like Ashbery, the interest of the poetry is in the movements of mentality and perception themselves, rather than in any identifiable subject or self to which they may be ascribed (though Crase doesn't hesitate to adopt a declamatory mode of expression when it seems called for by the scale of the poem).

The result is a poetry that bears the unmistakable marks of Ashbery's style and cast of mind yet which does not seem at all imitative. What Crase does in a way is receive Ashbery into the body of American poetry that is the common property of all poets, rather than let his work remain the private preserve of those who feel a tempermental affinity with it or have some special relation to it. In particular, he recovers Whitman through Ashbery—or, put another way, he enlists the rhetorical and psychological strategies of the poet many castigate as our most private and hermetic in the service of a public, Emersonian project of reclamation of his own—a Bloomian swerve implausible enough to render almost believable the claim that, even while "the past / Seems to be level in its place there's room for more / And the ragged additions polish the previous days."[7] And his example is powerful enough to make me think that the full measure of John Ashbery's influence on American poetry has yet to emerge.

## NOTES

1. Karl Marx and Friedrich Engels, *The Communist Manifesto,* ed. Samuel H. Beer (New York: Appleton-Century Crofts, 1955), 13.

2. The phrase is from Paavo Haavikko's "Winter Palace," *Selected Poems,* trans. Anselm Hollo (New York: Grossman, 1966), a poem that Ashbery has suggested may well be one of the century's great poems.

3. Allen Grossman, *Against Our Vanishing* (Boston: Rowan Tree Press, 1981), 49.

4. "Clepsydra," in John Ashbery, *Rivers and Mountains* (New York: Holt, Rinehart and Winston, 1966).

5. Ibid.

6. My remarks here on the development of subjectivity owe much to Jonathan Lear's *Love and Its Place in Nature* (New York: Farrar, Straus and Giroux, 1990).

7. Douglas Crase, "The Revisionist," *The Revisionist* (Boston: Little, Brown, 1981).

# Prose Poems and Poet's Prose
## *(1993)*

In *A Tradition of Subversion: The Prose Poem in English from Wilde to Ashbery* (Amherst: University of Massachusetts Press, 1992) Margueritte S. Murphy argues that certain anomalous works in prose constitute a distinctive genre—or "anti-genre"—whose "poeticity" (an unhappy word) is established by subverting the norms of conventional narrative, descriptive, and contemplative prose. It was inaugurated in France by Aloysius Bertrand and Baudelaire, and its practitioners there included Rimbaud, Lautremont, and Henri de Regnier. Stuart Merrill's collection of translations, *Pastels in Prose* (1890), introduced it to English audiences, and it flourished briefly in such examples of late-nineteenth-century decadence as Ernest Dowson's *Decorations in Prose* (1899) and Wilde's *Poems in Prose* (1894). The received view is that the genre did not transplant well into English, in part because the foil of the rigid French prosadic tradition was missing and also because the public reaction against decadence and aestheticism following Wilde's downfall reduced it to marginal status. The genre appeared thereafter only occasionally—in Eliot's early symbolist period, for example ("Hysteria," 1915), and more recently in the works of surrealist-influenced American poets like Michael Benedikt, Robert Bly, and W. S. Merwin. Yet Murphy's claim is that the real impulse behind the prose poem did not dissipate but continued to inform the writings of such high modernists as Williams and Stein and contemporary works like John Ashbery's *Three Poems* (1972) and Rob-

---

Originally appeared as "Review of Margueritte S. Murphy, 'A Tradition of Subversion: The Prose Poem in English from Wilde to Ashbery,' " *Modernism/Modernity* 1, no. 1 (Jan. 1994). Copyright © 1994 Johns Hopkins University Press.

ert Creely's *Presences: A Text for Marisol* (1976) (though Murphy does not discuss the latter). This impulse is contestatory: the true mark of the prose poem is not the brevity, closure, and interiority of its decadent instances but, rather, the attempt to undermine and mock the idea of fixed genres—in particular, those of narrative and discursive prose—as well as the social, sexual, and political conventions associated with fixed genres. Thus Dowson's poems parody the fairy tale and Wilde's the biblical parable (though the prose poem of Murphy's title is his notorious letter to Lord Alfred Douglas). The fragmentary and unpredictable character of Williams's *Kora in Hell: Improvisations* (1918) frustrates the reader's expectations and the provincialism said to underlie them; Stein's *Tender Buttons* (1914) disrupts English syntax and plays against such models of women's prose as cookbooks, etiquette manuals, and fashion magazines; and Ashbery's *Three Poems* subverts the contemplative meditation by resisting philosophical closure and rendering the idea of the writing and thinking subject problematic.

Though many of Murphy's discussions of particular writers are interesting (e.g., of Stein and women's writing and of Ashbery's pronomial vagaries), the book as a whole seems unconvincing, largely because of the strategy of its underlying argument. It posits a classification that encompasses far more than the prose poems derived from the original French model—a classification that is then declared, not too surprisingly, to be problematic. Since the examples given of this expanded genre have so few substantive qualities in common, the poeticity they are presumed to share must then be characterized negatively, by contrasting them with a stereotypical model of "normal" prose. Yet the conceptions of both prose and poetry adduced in this argument are too tidy and simple to accommodate much of the literature of modernism and its aftermath.

First, the model of normal prose Murphy posits strikes me as a fantasy. The aim of rhetoric at least since Quintilian has been to expand the affective capabilities of language by calculated departures from the straightforwardly declarative. The period under discussion is marked at its inception by the introspective ruminations of such "great prose brooders"[1] as James and Proust and encompasses both the Kantian speculations of

*A Man without Qualities* and the "novels" of Ronald Firbank. One need only reflect on the fact (mentioned by Murphy) that the same issues of the *Little Review* in which parts of *Kora in Hell* first appeared also contained excepts from *Ulysses* to find the dichotomy between conventional and subverted prose somewhat tendentious. Murphy counts *Tender Buttons* as a prose poem because of its radical syntactical disruptions; yet its style is a continuation of the concluding mode of Stein's *A Long Gay Book* (1911–12), which starts out as an exhaustive study of personality types.[2] And the preeminent work of this century written in the contemplative prose that Ashbery's *Three Poems* is said to subvert, Wittgenstein's *Philosophical Investigations,* not only lacks both ordinary argumentative structure and philosophical closure but also, in its interlocutory style, dispenses with a single meditative voice.

Second, the conception of poetry with which both normal prose and the prose poem is contrasted seems at odds with the development of Anglo-American poetry from the late nineteenth century to the present. Murphy appears to endorse the peculiarly French idea, derived from Mallarmé, that language in verse aspires to a purity that severs it from referentiality, and Mikhail Bakhtin's insistence that in lyric poetry it loses all connection with specific contexts, speech mannerisms, individual images, and worldviews. Yet one of the most conspicuous aspects of the development of poetry in English since Whitman—or since Wordsworth or Shakespeare, for that matter—is its incorporation of the discursive cadences of prose, along with the quotidian and demystified world such measures call to mind. "The Waste Land" is, as Helen Vendler has observed, a lyric and phantasmagoric self-portrait composed of images drawn from across history;[3] and by *Four Quartets* Eliot has appropriated not only F. H. Bradley's philosophical deconstruction of temporality but a discursive style often indistinguishable from prose as well. Marianne Moore's poetry is defiantly unaccentual and contains large elements of verbal collage. And as Stevens's work progresses it becomes increasingly difficult to distinguish his accentual from his unaccented verse.

Third, the intellectual sensibility both of writers of the kinds of works under discussion and of the audiences responsive to them tends to be one that is fretful about the workings of language generally (not just in particular genres) and of any sharp distinction between imaginative writing, on the one hand, and theoretical or critical reflection about it, on the other. Whether one sympathizes with the blurring of this particular distinction or not, it does make it hard to characterize the difference between a work like *Three Poems* and the theoretical writing it is supposed to undermine in a way that is liable to command widespread assent.

It seems to me that theoretically tinged texts devoid of lineation such as *Three Poems* are more accurately characterized by Stephen Fredman's notion of "poet's prose" than by the proposal that they constitute a distinctive, contestatory poetic genre.[4] Consider *Three Poems*. Most of its prose antecedents are already anomalous to various degrees, including de Chirico's novel *Hebdomeros* (1929), in which tableaux reminding one of nothing so much as his metaphysical paintings succeed each other in a limitless progression; and Caliban's speech to the audience in Auden's "The Sea and the Mirror" (1944), itself an imitation of James. It has affinities with Robert Walser's ambulatory musings in "The Walk" (1917) and in its headlong rush of self-explanation even resembles (to my mind) Wilde's *De Profundis* (1905). It is also of a piece with Ashbery's lineated long poems: it is followed shortly by "Self-Portrait in a Convex Mirror" (1974), and his visual image of the poem, which Murphy cites, of an opaque artifact of words is similar to an image he used earlier to describe "Clepsydra" (1966).[5] Like these other poems, it is a meditation on the necessity and impossibility of self-representation, and its repeated sense of false climax or conclusion, which Murphy takes to be subversive of the closure provided by traditional contemplative prose, is also a portrayal of the experience of "always cresting into one's present" (the phrase is from "Self-Portrait"), which is a recurrent theme throughout Ashbery's work.

A more general difficulty, which is fairly widespread in current theory, is a simplistic and condescending attitude towards literary modernism. Murphy identifies it with the academy, an association that only becomes plausible after New Criticism's infiltration of English departments in the 1940s and 1950s, long after most of modernism's original impulse had been spent. She takes the prose poem to be a paradigmatic postmodern genre, where the conception of the postmodern is Jean-François Lyotard's of "the unpresentable in presentation"—the implication being that, though the contents of modernist works were often transgressive, they remained well within the framework of recognizable forms, a framework abandoned by postmodern writers. Yet *Tender Buttons* and *Kora in Hell* were both written prior to 1920, and many of the ideas to be found in the more theoretically charged quarters of contemporary writing (Language poetry's obsession with the materiality of language, e.g.) were articulated earlier in the century (in this instance by the Objectivists of the 1930s). It seems to me that much recent quasi-philosophical theorizing about the literature of the last hundred years or so depends on generalizations and dichotomies that are simply too tidy to capture the unruly course it has taken in that period.

## NOTES

1. The apt phrase is Mary Kinzie's in "Thick and Thin," *American Poetry Review* 14 (Nov.–Dec. 1985).

2. Ulla E. Dydo, *A Stein Reader* (Evanston, IL: Northwestern University Press, 1993).

3. Helen Vendler, "*The Waste Land* Revisited," *Yale Review* 79 (winter 1990).

4. Stephen Fredman, *Poet's Prose: The Crisis in American Verse,* 2d ed. (Cambridge: Cambridge University Press, 1990).

5. David Shapiro, *John Ashbery: An Introduction to the Poetry* (New York: Columbia University Press, 1979).

# Poetry and the Experience
# of Experience
## *(1993)*

It used to be a truism that in the wake of romanticism poetry bore an essential relation, however vexed and problematic, to individual experience. If this is no longer quite the truism it once was, it is in part because of a general distaste for essentialism and in part because the idea that works of art are constituted by their creation has been replaced, at least in some quarters, by the idea that they are constituted by the social processes governing their reception and recognition. Yet even if one is sympathetic to this outlook, it seems to me to remain obviously true that subjective experience plays a central and irreducible role in how poems come into existence and in what they are taken to be. Just why this "obvious" truth should be so important is a question that deserves attention, and I shall turn to it later. But the more immediate problem, I think, is that the conception of experience employed by many of those who take it as dogma that poetry aims at its presentation—as well as by many who regard this as simply another version of "the naive vision of the individual creator"[1]—is such an attenuated and impoverished one that it is hardly surprising that it tends to be either sentimentally embraced or knowingly dismissed.

Another late truism is that poetry aims at a *representation* of experience. While some of the skepticism that this claim now

Also appears in *Where Theory Works: Essays on the Experience of Literature,* ed. Mary Kinzie (Evanston, IL: Northwestern University Press, forthcoming). I am grateful to Mary Kinzie, Douglas Crase, and the 1993–94 Fellows of the Center for Twentieth Century Studies, University of Wisconsin–Milwaukee for invaluable suggestions and discussions.

evokes stems from the anxiety that has come to surround the very idea of representation, mimetic conceptions of art have always occasioned a certain unease. Johnson's famous pronouncement, in the *Preface to Shakespeare,* that poetry ought to furnish "just representations of general nature" is followed shortly by his admission that Shakespeare's "adherence to general nature has exposed him to the censure of critics who form their judgements upon narrower principles"; and he goes on to mention Voltaire and several others as examples of critics who fault his depiction of royal subjects for incorporating elements of the comic and the vulgar.[2] It seems to me that one's attitude towards the claim that the representation of experience, or "general nature," is central to the poetic enterprise depends, to a great extent, on what one takes representation and experience to be. And here again, I think that much of the current distrust of this claim derives from narrow and simplistic conceptions of both.

There isn't a single explanation for the impoverished notion of experience that informs so much contemporary poetics and theory and no single form that its attenuation takes. Poetry, in its current state, is itself inhospitable to the discursive and the reflective, in part because of the widespread acceptance of what Mary Kinzie calls "the rhapsodic fallacy"—the assumption, which stems from certain strands in romanticism (though I think only *certain* strands), that poetry aims at "an ecstatic and unmediated self-consumption in the moment of perception and feeling."[3] Neopragmatism is another and more theoretical source of bias against the abstract and reflective aspects of subjective consciousness, since in its aversion to anything that hints at the transcendental it tends to discount the dimensions of experience that encourage certain traditional conceptions of representation and objectivity. Of course there are many more theoretical tendencies working *against* notions of subjectivity that emphasize its phenomenological or qualitative aspects—for not only are these difficult to fit into even the most plausible functionalist or structuralist accounts of mentality and agency; worse, ways of thinking about art that treat such aspects as central are often regarded as naive or ideologically suspect (though whether this is because of the theoretical recalcitrance of the phenomenological or because of the social significance these views actually have is something usually left unclear). And the culminative effect of these conflicting assumptions, allegiances, and suspicions is to foster the idea—an idea that is seldom made explicit—that many of the most familiar elements of human experience are unimportant or illusory or unreal.

What *does* experience actually encompass, and why should its representation matter? I shall try next to describe what I take to be the range of the subjective and what I think are some of the motives behind the many forms of its denial. I shall then indulge in some speculation about its importance and value and about the importance and value of its depiction. And I'll end by proposing that one way poetry seeks to capture it is through the enactment of a version of the Kantian experience of the sublime.

## The Scope of Experience

Early in the *Second Meditation* Descartes frames the question "What then am I?" and he immediately answers, "A conscious being . . . that doubts, understands, asserts, denies, is willing, is unwilling; [and] has sense and imagination." The experience enjoyed by such a being is the awareness of what the seventeenth century called "ideas," which Locke characterized as "whatsoever the mind perceives in itself, or is the immediate object of perception, thought or understanding."[4] One doesn't have to follow Descartes in separating the experiencing subject from the body, or follow the theory of ideas in reifying the contents of consciousness, in order to equate experience with subjective awareness and to identify its range with whatever that awareness can include.

Its range includes sensation and emotion. While part of my reason for surveying it is to combat the appeal of the rhapsodic fallacy of reducing experience to perception and feeling, one can hardly deny the vividness with which these can occupy and even dominate the field of consciousness or the defining links they bear to such other modes of experience as desire, belief, and intention. Vivid as they are, though, neither sensations nor emotions are subjectively simple. Perception used to be thought of as a passive process, unadulterated by conceptualization or inference, in which a variety of "sensible qualities" were made directly available to the mind.[5] But with the demise of this "myth of the given," or "myth of presence," the relation between perception and the more abstract or reflective forms of cognition has become increasingly problematic. And since there is also a complementary tendency to locate sensation in its relation to the satisfaction of desire, it is important to remember as well the disinterested forms of perception involved in what Kant called judgments of taste, or in the invasion of sensation by memory—the perception of an "autumnal" slant of light, or the experience of Proustian recollection, when a current sensation awakens the bodily traces of an earlier one and brings about an awareness of the gulf of time that separates them.

Affective experience too is less tidy than it was once taken to be. Descartes thought of emotions as passive and took these "passions" to be a species of perception—namely, the soul's perception of certain "commotions" taking place in the body.[6] Yet as with perception, it has become commonplace to ascribe a cognitive dimension to the emotions and to see the distinction between them and nonaffective states like belief and imagination as less crisp than it once appeared. And while there is still a tendency to link emotions to thoughts about the kinds of concrete situations that impinge more or less directly on our appetites and desires, Eliot's suggestion "that what is often held to be a capacity for abstract thought, in a poet, is a capacity for abstract feeling" is one I have long found intriguing, and I want to come back to later.[7]

Since visceral emotions such as excitement and fear are often associated with the gratification or frustration of desire by sensation, or the experience of bodily pleasure or pain, it is salutary to remember that the range of desire extends well beyond those satisfiable by sensation, or perceptions of the passive sort, to include desires concerning virtually every aspect of experience—the wish that idle curiosity be satisfied or that inquiry broaden the scope and coherence of one's beliefs about the natural order or that various designs involving one-self and others be realized. Even more general are desires occasioned by the Socratic question "How should I live?"—desires that one's life go a certain way or that one's experience as a whole have a certain character. These desires are in-formed by self-awareness and a conception of oneself as a person, and among the most important of them are those higher-order desires—which Harry Frankfurt has done so much to illuminate—about our own wants and preferences: for instance, that they be different than they are or that they become ineffective or that they maintain themselves and shape our conduct.[8] I think that Frankfurt is right to suggest that that most central and puzzling aspect of experience—the conception and experience of oneself as a "free" agent—has less to do with a belief in one's exemption from the natural order than with a delicate equilibrium between the higher-order desires about the kind of person one would like to be and the desires one would like to have, on the one hand, and the wants and preferences that actually prompt one to act, on the other.

Desires prompt actions in conjunction with beliefs, and be-liefs and the concepts they involve are parts of subjective ex-perience too. Crude empiricist models tie beliefs tightly to perception—for Hume, for example, a belief is a particularly vivid idea, an idea that itself is just the trace of an earlier sense-impression—and tend to treat as illusory beliefs and concepts that can't be easily retraced to perception. Yet although beliefs produced and sustained by the experience of the senses have an obvious force, and while the concepts they embody are ones of which our grasp often seems especially sure, it seems unde-niable that the scope of our opinions and of our ability to form concepts ranges far beyond them. I am thinking here not just of beliefs about the unobservable and the abstract but also, as in the case of desire, of higher-order thoughts that take beliefs and concepts themselves as objects of experience and reflec-tion. For we don't merely *have* sensations, thoughts, and the other forms of experience; we have also the capacity for an awareness or experience *of* them and for conceiving of them as constituting a single field of awareness. Hume, in a well-known passage, confessed that "when I enter most intimately into what I call *myself*, I always stumble on some particular perception or other, of heat or cold, light or shade, love or hatred, pain or pleasure"; but that "I can never catch *myself*."[9] He concluded that the notion of the self was in some sense illusory. But I think that Hume was misguided in searching for the self among the objects of experience and that Kant was more nearly correct in tracing the notion to the awareness of the unity of experience, to "the representation of that to which all thinking stands in relation."[10] For somehow we *do* manage to form a conception of a self comprising a single field of awareness and to think of it as standing in some sort of relation, however problematic, to a larger context—to the "world" if you like—which includes but isn't exhausted by the experiences through which that field of awareness is constituted.

It is this sort of self-consciousness that gives rise, I believe, to notions like representation, truth, and objectivity. For it is our awareness *of* our sensations, thoughts, and desires, together with our capacity to conceive of them as aspects of a self embedded in some broader context, that allows us to frame the question of their relation to that world. And to try to situate experience in this way is to start to think of it as, in a very broad sense, representational—as leading us to form conceptions of its surrounding context that can be accurate or inaccurate, or as satisfied or frustrated, by that context. It is sometimes suggested that representational conceptions of thought are merely a stage in the development of a Western philosophical tradition that has pretty much exhausted its usefulness. It *is* true that most attempts to systematically articulate exactly what the representation of the world involves have turned out to be artifacts of particular intellectual moments— Wittgenstein's "picture theory" of the *Tractatus* being one of the more notorious examples. But it strikes me as just perverse to suppose that the roots of the idea that thought can be about the world, and is capable of representing it with varying degrees of accuracy, are to be found in the philosophy section of the local university library, rather than in that conception of subjective experience as embedded in a larger context to which our capacity for self-awareness gives rise.

It is also this conception that allows us to think of ourselves and our experiences in two different and perhaps irreconcilable ways—from what Thomas Nagel calls a "subjective" or "internal" perspective and from an "external" or "objective" one (even though *thinking* of experience in either of these ways is itself part of subjective experience).[11] To think of experience subjectively is to be aware of its "qualitative" aspect—of "what it's like" to *have* a sensation, to *experience* a strong emotion or desire, or to engage in conscious reflection about the range of thought. Calling this perspective internal suggests that it's available only to those whose experiences they are. Yet given that we can form a conception of ourselves and our experience as part of a larger context whose nature is independent of experience and thought, we can also attempt to think of these in the way we seem able to think of other aspects of that world—as they are in themselves, apart from how they are presented to our awareness. Of course we can't actually *adopt* this "view from Nowhere"—for to think of the world at all is to think of it from whatever position we happen to occupy. Talk of a view from Nowhere is simply a vivid way of describing the fact that it is part of our experience itself that we can form an imaginative conception of a world whose nature is independent of our thought and to which we belong. And the expansion of our knowledge of the world has been basically a matter of filling in the details of this conception.

Yet when we try to think of *ourselves* in this way, the effort seems to remain incomplete. The qualitative dimensions of experience that appear so vivid from an internal perspective, and the importance and significance with which we invest our feelings and desires, seem to evaporate when we try to think of ourselves objectively, as part of the natural order. This appearance of incompleteness could of course be illusory, and we could become convinced that the intuition that certain important aspects of experience defy inclusion in an objective conception of the world is simply mistaken. Or it may be, as Nagel thinks, that the subjective and objective conceptions of ourselves and the world are both necessary and necessarily partial. I'm inclined to believe that Nagel is right, though I have no idea how to argue the point. In either case, though, it does

seem a feature of subjective experience as presently consti-
tuted that it allows us to form compelling but radically differ-
ent conceptions of its character and significance.

This survey is partial. The notion of experience that in-
forms contemporary poetry seems so hostile to abstraction
that I've concentrated on its conceptual (as opposed to what
might be called its Dionysian) aspects. But I want to turn now
to some of the impulses that encourage restricted notions of
experience in literary and philosophical studies generally.

The survey I have given consists of characterizations of
various varieties of conscious thought. There is a widespread
tendency to treat descriptions like these as parts of a *theory,* a
theory subject to interpretation, revision, or outright rejec-
tion. In literary studies this usually means regarding the con-
cepts such descriptions involve—concepts like belief, desire,
emotion, the self, and representation—as historically condi-
tioned social constructions or as manifestations of underlying
psychoanalytic structures and mechanisms. In cognitive stud-
ies it amounts to regarding them as hypotheses—parts of
"folk psychology," or what Daniel Dennett calls "heterophe-
nomenology"[12]—to be accepted to the extent that they can be
instantiated by neurophysiological processes and states that
mirror their causal structure. Yet all this is to transform the
field of awareness into a kind of *text* and to treat one's relation
to experience on the model of reading, or of having certain
propositional attitudes. And it seems to me that none of these
approaches is able to accommodate what makes conscious ex-
perience interesting in the first place—its qualitative char-
acter, or the fact that there is something that it's *like* to have it.
This, of course, is a matter of ongoing controversy and isn't
going to be resolved soon. But I think that one of the motives
for downplaying certain aspects of subjective experience is a
commitment to theoretical models of mentality that, to my
mind at least, remain largely speculative.

The impulses combined in certain forms of neopragma-
tism—particularly the form articulated by Richard Rorty—
supply another motive for circumscribing the domain of expe-
rience.[13] Pragmatists urge us to think of the formation and
revision of our beliefs, concepts, and values not as a matter of

assessing them with regard to a priori standards of rationality but, rather, as an ongoing effort to adapt them to our interests and experience broadly construed; and to discard as idle those concepts and distinctions that play no role in this effort. Now surely there is something right about this. "Coherence with experience," broadly construed, *must* be our ultimate standard of assessment, since it is our *only* standard of assessment—for to think about anything at all is to think about it from whatever position we happen to occupy as subjects of experience. Yet Rorty combines pragmatism in this broad sense with an antipathy to philosophical traditions that incorporate certain conceptions of knowledge, representation, truth, and objectivity, or a sharp distinction between the world and our representations of it. I suggested earlier that these notions themselves arise from our experience of self-consciousness and from our ability to form an imaginative idea of ourselves and of our experience as parts of a world that is independent of them. But if so, a sweeping dismissal of these notions is bound to lead to a denigration of those aspects of subjective experience that give rise to them—in particular, the experience of forming a self-image that incorporates the idea of a view from Nowhere. This is not, of course, the rhapsodic fallacy's simple-minded self-extinction in a swoon of sensation. Nevertheless, it seems to me that Rorty's pragmatic allegiance to experience, combined with his hostility to a certain theoretical stance, encourages a conception of experience that works to validate that antipathy.

Rorty's considered view is more subtle. It isn't that the familiar concepts and questions of philosophy have no roots at all in subjective experience—for how could they fail to?—but that we'd be *better off* without them or if our experience were somehow reshaped to eliminate them.[14] Better off in what way, though? Well, less fretful or less anxious or less prone to waste our intellectual and emotional resources on "fruitless, irresolvable disagreements on dead-end issues"—or, in a word, happier. Yet what an odd conception of happiness! Whatever it is, happiness surely has more to do with a view of one's life as a whole, and the development and exercise of the capacities one has in the course of that life—what Aristotle called *eudaimonia,* or "flourishing"—than with a mere absence of anxiety and the restriction of one's desires and interests to the most readily satisfied. If the capacity for reflective self-awareness leads us to think of ourselves in irreconcilable ways, why are we better off for ceasing to exercise it? This is the question of the value of experience and its representation, to which I now turn.

## Why It Matters What It's Like

Why is subjective experience so important? Perhaps the peculiarity of the question is mitigated by the reflection that the subjective has assumed the mantle of contemporary theory's Other, a specter to be exorcised as "a mere residuum alongside the desiring machines," or as a by-product of "the opposition of the forces of attraction and repulsion."[15] The merits of these structuralist deflations, and their functionalist counterparts, strike me as less important than their place in that vast cloud of anxiety and allegiance that has come to surround the whole notion of subjectivity. And this raises the question of why it should have seemed to matter so much in the first place—matter in its own right, or as an object of representation generally, or as an object of poetic representation.

I think the answer lies in its connection with moral value. Attempts to distinguish the loose set of judgments, injunctions, and prohibitions that constitute the domain of the ethical from mere customs and patterns of behavior invariably connect it in one way or another with the subjective. The significance of this connection depends, of course, on one's attitude towards the moral. And just as there are deflationary attitudes towards subjectivity, there are strains of thought that are dismissive of moral notions too. Yet just as with subjectivity—perhaps even more so—tendencies like these strike me as theoretical fantasies, fantasies in which one tries to float free of one's actual experience and behavior. For I think that the whole idea of importance, or "mattering," is finally a moral one, central to our self-image, that rests on the notion of a subjective life.

Different conceptions of the moral appeal to subjectivity in different ways. The crudest forms of utilitarianism take ethical injunctions and prohibitions to rest on the relation of conduct to sensations like pleasure and pain. Subtler forms take moral conduct to aim at the promotion of welfare, or the satisfaction of interests—where interests are something like considered desires that one identifies as one's own. Hume thought that morality rested on the experience of sympathy for the experience of others, while Kantian conceptions are based on a respect for persons as intrinsically valuable and an idea of reciprocity—for since each person is worthy of respect, to act morally is to act in ways that would be acceptable from the other's point of view. Here the appeal to subjectivity lies in the thought that people *have* points of view—subjective ones—from which courses of conduct can be appraised. But all these conceptions assume that human conduct impinges on people's experience and that it makes a difference to what life is like *for* them. Without this assumption, the idea that people *have* interests—let alone the idea of considering the world from another person's viewpoint—makes no more sense than the notion of ascribing interests to a fire hydrant or of considering the world from its particular perspective. This isn't to say that all that matters morally is subjective experience, since people have interests ranging well beyond it. But without subjective viewpoints, could there even be interests at all? Could a desiring machine's desires actually matter, if they made no difference from anyone's perspective? A landscape can't have interests, though it can be an interest of *mine*. But this is only because it can matter to me.

So far I've been speaking of the subjective too ingenuously, for it is, I think, problematic in ways that lead to the issue of its representation. Representation is a notion that lends itself to caricature, and I want to caution against models that limit it to description or resemblance while leaving open for now the question of how poetry might accomplish a representation of experience. What seems so problematic about subjectivity is its *tenuous* character—or, since that way of putting it sounds oxymoronic, its *lack* of an objective nature. Sometimes this lack is emblematized by its evanescence—certainly one of its arresting characteristics and one that leads to a complementary view of art as an attempt to preserve the ephemeral. Yet the deeper aspect of its tenuousness isn't the perishability it shares with wildflowers and mayflies but what might be called its "viewpoint dependence."

I said earlier that experience includes the ability to form an objective conception of the world and of one's place in it— where *objective* here means something like "as it really is, apart from how it appears to us or how we conceive of it." The development of natural science can be seen as the elaboration of this conception; and what Nagel has made so vivid is the difficulty—even, one begins to suspect, the impossibility—of incorporating the subjective within it. For while it seems easy to speculate about the nature of regions of time and space remote from our experience, it seems hard, if not impossible, to make sense of wondering what the "nature" of one's experience might actually be—what it really is, apart from how it strikes one or apart from one's apprehension of it. The conspicuous features of interiority are difficult to locate in the landscape of the objective, and if we equate that landscape with the real, we might be tempted to say that such aspects don't literally exist; or be tempted by the "false objectification" of simply expanding our inventory of the world's furniture to include the recalcitrant features of consciousness.[16] I think the right course, though, is to resist both of these temptations and to try to think of the "reality" of the subjective as something constituted by its apprehension, or by its status as a focus of awareness. And since to speak about apprehension or awareness is to speak, in a very broad way, about representation, the point could also be put by saying that subjective experience only exists insofar as it can be represented; or that, apart from our representations of it, this central aspect of our self-image isn't real at all.

Allen Grossman, whom I think of as poetry's most fertile current theoretician, has described poetry's central function as "the keeping of the image of persons as precious in the world" and has characterized poetic speech as a "portrait of the inner and invisible (intuitional) person." While I'm not entirely comfortable with the categorical tone, I believe that the substantive view of the relation between poetry and experience contained in these remarks is basically the same as the one I am trying to develop here. What Grossman means by *person* is a Kantian subject of experience and a rational will, a "being whose existence in itself is an end"; and it seems to me that to say that experience, in the sense I have tried to capture, matters is simply to say that persons—whom Grossman also describes as art's "underlying term or value"—matter. Where I have spoken of the importance of poetry's representation of experience, he locates its value in the preservation of the human image, in its ability to present a portrait of the "inner and invisible," and in its "ontological affirmation . . . : Here is a person." But the question now is how poetry might manage to accomplish this.[17]

### Revisiting the Sublime

Representation is a broad and unruly notion, tied in various ways to such other notions as reference, resemblance, causation, simulation, expression, metaphor, metonomy, evocation, depiction, and performance. One of our century's important philosophical lessons, I believe, is the negative one that questions about the essential nature of representation are misconceived—which is one reason why discussions of cultural, aesthetic, and philosophical issues that turn on critiques of representation so often seem to attack a series of straw men. Attempts to delimit the scope of genuine representation almost invariably wind up acknowledging a complementary domain that undercuts the "real" one, as with Wittgenstein's distinction between what can be said and what can only be shown; or the logical positivists' distinction between language that is cognitively meaningful and that which is merely emotive or expressive; or New Criticism's distinction between the semantic properties intrinsic to a literary text and those that are irrelevant interpolations into it.

All this is by way of disavowing anything resembling a systematic theory of the poetic representation of experience. Reading a poem (and here I use *reading* advisedly, since the dimension of poetry I am trying to characterize emerges more clearly in reading poems than in hearing them) is itself an experience; and to speak of poetry's "representation" of experience, in the broad sense I have in mind, is to speak of an experience of a certain sort that can be induced by reading a poem. The particular sort of experience I mean is a higher-order one involving the thought or awareness—the experience, if you like—of the range of subjectivity as such, and of its precarious relation to the world in which it is situated, which it nevertheless manages to reflect.

In the third *Critique* Kant introduces the notion of what he calls the "dynamical sublime" to describe a particular train of thought or experience that occurs in the presence of natural phenomena of gigantic scale or magnitude. Confronted with a vast physical presence—in the eighteenth century the experience was associated with the Alps, tours of which had recently become fashionable; though something like the Grand Canyon or the St. Louis Arch would do as well—one first feels overwhelmed at the thought of the disparity between one's own physical stature and the natural immensity before one. Yet this very thought of a *vast* magnitude, by comparison with which one seems limited to the point of insignificance, leads to the thought of an *unbounded* or *infinite* magnitude. And "since in contrast to this standard everything in nature is small"—including the overpowering Alp—the mind is led to an awareness of its "superiority over nature itself in its immensity."[18] For the ability to form a conception of an unbounded magnitude, which isn't to be found in nature, enables us to think of all of nature as "small" and to conceive of ourselves, the subjects of that conception, as distinct from and "above" it. Kant is quick to remark that on the surface "this principle seems far-fetched and the result of some subtle reasoning"; nevertheless, he thinks that "even the commonest judging can be based on [it], even though we are not always conscious of it." Moreover, I think that the oscillations of thought and self-awareness that he describes in characterizing the dynamical sublime can be abstracted from his overt concern with physical immensity and the mind's superiority to nature to characterize the kind of experience involved in the poetic representation of subjectivity.

In an early essay Nagel tried to characterize the sense in which human life might be thought to be "absurd" along the following lines.[19] Each of us has a "personal" perspective on his or her own life, from which we can't help but regard that life and its interests and concerns with tremendous seriousness; and which invests them with an importance informing almost every aspect of our deliberation and practical reasoning. Yet each of us is also capable of self-awareness and of mentally "stepping back" and regarding that life and its concerns from an impersonal perspective, *sub specie aeternitatis*—a perspective from which those concerns seem to have no real importance or significance at all. And since this is true no matter what our interests may be, there is a ridiculous but inescapable discrepancy between the importance with which we invest our lives and our projects and the importance we realize them to actually possess. One possible response—a response Nagel associates with Camus and dismisses as romantic—would be the affirmative one of adopting an attitude of defiance towards a world one knows to be indifferent to one's life. Nagel's own response, which strikes me as equally romantic and redemptive (though none the worse for that), is to think of our appreciation of life's absurdity as a manifestation of our most "advanced and interesting characteristic," "the capacity to transcend ourselves in thought."[20]

Leaving aside the issues of superiority, affirmation, and redemption, the important thing to notice is the structural similarity between Kant's characterization of the experience of the sublime and Nagel's description of the apprehension of the absurd. Both share a characteristic trajectory of experience, which starts with an unreflective conception of oneself and attitude towards one's experience; followed by an awareness of something inhuman or impersonal (a vast physical presence, a conception of the world *sub specie aeternitatis*), by contrast with which the self and its experiences are rendered problematic and radically diminished; followed finally by the higher-order reflection that this whole chain of apprehension and realization is itself part of the range of subjectivity. There is of course a difference between Kant's optimistic attitude towards this trajectory and Nagel's pessimistic one. But what strikes me as significant isn't so much the outcome of the sequence of shifts between viewpoints—from the subjective to the impersonal and back to the subjective again—as the oscillation itself, "the rhythm of the series of repeated jumps" (in John Ashbery's words from "The Skaters"),[21] "from abstract into positive and back to a slightly less diluted abstract."

For what seems most characteristic of subjectivity—and what allows for the possibility of its poetic representation—isn't the content of any particular state of awareness but, rather, the transitions from instant to instant between perspectives, from an awareness of the objects of thought to an awareness of thought itself, in an unbounded sequence of reflexive movements. The poetry of subjectivity is sometimes associated with privileged conditions of consciousness, simple or elevated. Yet both the rhapsodic fallacy's unselfconscious phenomenology as well as the Kantian sublime's transcendent perception of nature as "small" (which coincides, incidentally, with what Wittgenstein termed "the mystical"—"feeling the world as a limited whole")[22] are just as much theoretical fantasies as the deflationary attitudes towards subjectivity and morality I touched on earlier. What isn't a fantasy, however, is something poetry is especially suited to engender in a heightened way—the vacillation in viewpoints from moment to moment, along with the larger movement between a personal perspective on the objects of one's attention and an objective view of oneself as part of an impersonal natural world.

Poetry has the resources (which it doesn't always draw on) to enact these oscillations: the imagistic and metaphoric potential to evoke perception and sensation; the discursive capacity of language to express states of propositional awareness and reflexive consciousness; the rhythmic ability to simulate the movement of thought across time; and a lyric density that can tolerate abrupt shifts in perspective and tone without losing coherence. This certainly isn't to say that poetry is *uniquely* capable of accomplishing this sort of enactment. Yet music, for instance, while it possesses the dynamical resources to follow the ebb and flow of subjectivity, lacks the discursive capacity to capture its content. Reflexivity and shifts in viewpoint are harder to achieve in painting, though not impossible. And while prose is also a medium well suited for the representation of the subjective, the movements and transitions characteristic of the conventional prose narrative are more gradual and extended than those of poetry, producing less an awareness of the shifts in perspective themselves than of how the novel's world appears from those different vantage points.

The arc of experience of the Kantian sublime comes to rest in the mind's realization of its transcendence of nature; while in Nagel's apprehension of the absurd it falters at the level of the impersonal surround. Yet another model that informs many poems defers the apotheosis, prolonging the oscillation between the subjective and the transcendent indefinitely. The trajectory of Wordsworth's *Prelude,* for example, is close to the Kantian one.[23] Early in book 2 the self becomes objectified in the recognition of

> The vacancy between me and those days
> Which yet have such self-presence in my mind,
> That, sometimes, when I think of it, I seem
> Two consciousnesses, conscious of myself
> And of some other Being.

In book 7 the self is dispersed by its immersion in the urban spectacle of London and Bartholomew Fair, culminating in the confrontation with the Blind Beggar, whose life is externalized in a written label pinned to his chest:

> and it seemed
> To me that in this Label was a type,
> Or emblem, of the utmost that we know,
> Both of ourselves and of the universe;
> And, on the shape of the unmoving man,
> His fixed face and sightless eyes, I look'd
> As if admonished from another world.

Yet the soul is recoverable, for the self's dispersal "is not wholly so to him who looks / In steadiness"; and the poem presses confidently on towards its closure in the soul's transcendence of nature through its perception of the world as a totality:

The universal spectacle throughout
Was shaped for admiration and delight,
Grand in itself alone, but in that breach
Through which the homeless voice of waters rose,
That dark deep thoroughfare, had Nature lodged
The soul, the imagination of the whole.

Contrast the trajectory of Wordsworth's poem with that of
John Ashbery's "Self-Portrait in a Convex Mirror."[24] Here the
self's confrontation with its externalization consists of a series
of approaches and withdrawals taking place in the urban con-
text of New York, "a logarithm / Of other cities." But the
movement towards identification is never completed, and at
the poem's end the image of the self's double falls back and
flattens into inertness, leaving it stranded in the city—"the
gibbous / Mirrored eye of an insect"—with the movement re-
maining only as a never-to-be-realized possibility, a "diagram
still sketched on the wind."

Or contrast Stevens's "Auroras of Autumn" with "An Ordi-
nary Evening in New Haven." "Auroras of Autumn" is our
century's great poem of the completed Kantian sublime, mov-
ing from a series of domestic interiors to an encounter with
nature on the scale of the northern lights, to an apotheosis in

This contrivance of the spectre of the spheres,
Contriving balance to contrive a whole,
The vital, the never-failing genius,
Fulfilling his meditations great and small.

How different the cosmic stability of this resolution seems
from the endless vacillations of "An Ordinary Evening in New
Haven" (the last of Stevens's major long poems), as the mind
roams back and forth between "The eye's plain version" and
"A recent imagining of reality," the "second giant [that] kills
the first." In canto 9 the attention shifts from what is seen to
the seeing "eye made clear of uncertainty," in an effort to
incorporate "Everything, the spirit's alchemicana / Included."
But the effort remains problematic, and one of the poem's
final celebrations is of the movement of subjectivity itself, "a

visibility of thought / In which hundreds of eyes, in one mind, see at once."

There are endless variations on this trajectory. Its completion can take a self-referentially aesthetic form, as in Marianne Moore's "An Octopus." Or the deflation of the familiar can be abrupt, as in the sudden and disorienting realization, in Elizabeth Bishop's "Over 2,000 Illustrations and a Complete Concordance," of "Everything only connected by 'and' and 'and' "; or it can take the form of a gradual withdrawal from the particularities of the individual life, as in Robert Pinsky's "At Pleasure Bay." But I find that the enactment of such movements takes place most convincingly in poems of a certain scale, which is one reason I associate it with, say, Ashbery's longer works—the prose of *Three Poems* or the lineated "Self-Portrait" and "Flow Chart"—and poems of James Schuyler's like "Hymn to Life" and "The Morning of the Poem," rather than with poems of a relatively brief round.

Yet the question still lingers of why one should care so much about poetry constructed on this model. A complaint often heard about contemporary verse is that it is excessively diffuse and subjective; and certainly there is something right about this complaint as it applies to the almost generic poem (usually short) distinguished by a vapid and unreflective self-absorption. Of course the subjectivity I have been concerned with here is richer and more complex; but one may reasonably wonder why poems embodying it should be more interesting on that account.

I said earlier that the importance of subjectivity and its poetic representation lies in its link with moral value. I still think that this answer is ultimately the right one, yet in a way it seems too remote from the experience of poetry to explain why certain poems seem engaging and moving. What is needed is an explanation at the affective level, and I want to return finally to that intriguing remark of Eliot's I mentioned a while ago—"that what is often held to be a capacity for abstract thought, in a poet, is a capacity for abstract feeling." What in the world could an "abstract feeling" be? For while I've always found the phrase an apt way of characterizing something about certain poems that draws me towards them, this isn't the same as understanding what that feature is.

The most widespread current model of feeling is a cognitive one that assimilates emotions to propositional attitudes. I suppose that on such a model an abstract emotion would simply be an emotion whose content was appropriately "abstract"—like, for instance, feeling elation at the proof of Fermat's Last Theorem. But I think that what Eliot had in mind was an "abstractness" intrinsic to the feeling itself and not merely to whatever it happened to be about; and here I find Descartes's picture of the passions, for all its shortcomings, more suggestive. Descartes thought of emotions as *internal* perceptions, as the awareness of various bodily "commotions"—the flow of "animal spirits" through the nerves, the constriction of the vessels about the heart, a tightening of the muscles—occasioned by external situations that have been found to give rise to such upheavals. Perhaps we can think of abstract feelings in much the same way—as the awareness of the subjective commotions of the reflexive movements of experience and of thought's oscillations between viewpoints, occasioned by situations that are themselves partially subjective. Surely this more nearly captures the experience of the Kantian sublime, which actually feels not so much like a metaphysical apprehension of the self's independence from the natural order, as like an affective transformation of the world. Or if one thinks, as I do, that our notions of freedom and autonomy ultimately derive from our capacity for higher-order reflection, one might call it *both* a metaphysical intuition and an affective transport. In any case, I think that what draws us to poetry that enacts the kind of representation of experience I have tried to describe is its ability to engender those powerful yet abstract feelings of which Eliot spoke; or, better, that this sort of poetry, like the experience on which it draws and which it helps sustain, matters because it moves.

## NOTES

1. Pierre Bourdieu, *The Field of Cultural Production: Essays on Art and Literature* (New York: Columbia University Press), 34.

2. Samuel Johnson, *Preface to Shakespeare* (1765), in *Selected Poetry and Prose,* ed. Frank Brady and W. K. Wimsatt (Berkeley: University of California Press, 1977), 301, 303.

3. Mary Kinzie, *The Cure of Poetry in an Age of Prose* (Chicago: University of Chicago Press, 1993), 1.

4. John Locke, *An Essay Concerning Human Understanding* (1690), bk. 2, chap. 8, sec. 8.

5. George Berkeley, *Three Dialogues between Hylas and Philonous* (1713), First Dialogue.

6. Descartes, *The Passions of the Soul* (1649).

7. T. S. Eliot, a talk on "Tradition and the Practice of Poetry" (1936), *Southern Review,* ed. A. Walton Litz, 21, no. 4 (Oct. 1985): 883.

8. Harry Frankfurt, *The Importance of What We Care About* (New York: Cambridge University Press, 1988).

9. David Hume, *A Treatise on Human Nature* (1739), bk. 1, pt. 4, sec. 6.

10. Immanuel Kant, *Prolegomena to Any Future Metaphysics* (1783), pt. 3, sec. 46.

11. Thomas Nagel, *The View from Nowhere* (New York: Oxford University Press, 1986); and *Mortal Questions* (New York: Cambridge University Press, 1979).

12. Paul Churchland, *Scientific Realism and the Plasticity of Mind* (New York: Cambridge University Press, 1979); Daniel Dennett, *Consciousness Explained* (Boston: Little, Brown, 1991).

13. Richard Rorty, *Objectivity, Relativism, and Truth* (New York: Cambridge University Press, 1991).

14. Rorty, "Putnam and the Relativist Menace," *Journal of Philosophy* 90, no. 9 (Sept. 1993): 457.

15. Gilles Deleuze and Felix Guattari, *Anti-Oedipius: Capitalism and Schizophrenia* (Minneapolis: University of Minnesota Press, 1983), 17, 19.

16. Nagel, *The View from Nowhere,* 86. But Nagel is ambivalent with regard to "property dualism," which merely adds qualitative properties to the world's real properties.

17. The quotations in this paragraph are from Allen Grossman, *The Sighted Singer* (Baltimore: Johns Hopkins University Press, 1992), 6, 306. The third quotation is Grossman's own citation from Kant's *Foundations of the Metaphysics of Morals* (1785), sec. 2.

18. The quotations in this paragraph are from Kant, *Critique of Judgment* (1790), bk. 2, sec. 28.

19. Nagel, "The Absurd," *Mortal Questions.*

20. Ibid., 23.

21. In John Ashbery, *Rivers and Mountains* (New York: Holt, Rinehart and Winston, 1966).

22. Ludwig Wittgenstein, *Tractatus Logico-Philosophicus* (1921; London: Routledge and Kegan Paul, 1961), 6:45.

23. All quotations are from the 1805 version of *The Prelude*. Neil Hertz discusses some of the following passages in chapters 3 and 10 of *The End of the Line: Essays on Psychoanalysis and the Sublime* (New York: Columbia University Press, 1985).

24. In John Ashbery, *Self-Portrait in a Convex Mirror* (New York: Viking, 1975).

# The Romance of Realism
## *(1996)*

In the *Crito* Socrates, his death imminent, asks of a piece of reasoning "whether this argument will appear in any way different to me in my present circumstances, or whether it remains the same"; and the clear implication of the question is that if a piece of reasoning is valid its force must remain unaffected by alterations in mood or outlook occasioned by changing circumstances. The pretension of philosophy to a passion for truth is traditionally taken to bar the influence of the passions on the way in which truth is pursued: a rational person's assessment of a philosophical argument or thesis must, so the tradition holds, be a disinterested one, in which considerations of temperament, inclination, and intuition have no proper role. On the whole, the effect of this tradition is salutary, bequeathing to philosophy a kind of integrity increasingly absent in other humanistic disciplines, an integrity perhaps purchased at the cost of a certain intellectual marginality.

Yet for a long time it has struck me that in practice philosophers depart considerably from this ideal, in that their attractions and aversions to particular views, problems, and arguments often seem inexplicable on rational (in some narrow sense of that term) grounds alone. When Wittgenstein spoke of a philosopher's suffering from a "loss of problems" he seemed to suggest an affective dimension to one's relation to philosophical issues, a suggestion that is certainly true to my experience of the discipline. Some issues that I find profoundly problematic and engaging—scepticism and the mind/body problem, for instance—others regard as quaint

From *New Literary History* 28, no. 4 (fall 1997). Reprinted by permission.

academic curiosities; and nowhere, it seems to me, do considerations of temperament play a greater role than in philosophers' attitudes toward the host of issues involved in the problem of philosophical realism. To some (including myself) *some* view that deserves the name *realism* seems obviously correct and beyond serious argument; to others the very word provokes something akin to an allergic reaction. This is all the more striking because the question of what realism and its denial actually involve is a rather subtle one, and it is often not at all clear, when someone passionately defends or denies it, just what is being passionately defended or denied.

Plato's opposition of philosophy to poetry was rooted in the conviction that poetry, whose persuasiveness derives from the vagaries of the passions rather than the force of impersonal argument, was an unfit vehicle for knowledge. I think that the popular idea that poetry ought to remain untainted by the discursive and the conceptual is an insidious one and that it has had a deleterious effect on the recent development of American poetry. Poetry can and should, I believe, approach experience and the world in full generality and embody stances or attitudes towards them that can only be called theoretical. Yet it is true that conceptualization in poetry does not call for impersonal rational justification; rather, it derives its force from the brute fact that the poet has found a particular way of situating himself and his experience in relation to the world compelling.

I want to suggest that something like this occurs in philosophy too and that there are deep affinities between certain positions or views that are properly thought of as philosophical and certain attitudes or outlooks that inform poetry at its most ambitious and powerful. What I want to suggest is a relation between realism and romanticism.

I. A. Richards, in *Coleridge on Imagination,* raised something like this issue but, because of a certain philosophical view about meaning that he held, declined to pursue it. Richards identified two doctrines and then raised the question of which of them Coleridge held and which was Wordsworth's:

In the first doctrine Man, through Nature, is linked with something other than himself which he perceives through her. In the second, he makes of her, as with a mirror, a transformed image of his own being.[1]

What Richards meant by the first doctrine is a form of realism (as I shall characterize it in a moment), in that it insists on a discontinuity between the world (what he calls "Nature") and ourselves. The second, which emphasizes the continuity between nature and ourselves, is akin to philosophical idealism. But rather than identify Wordsworth or Coleridge with either of these views, he held that their apparent incompatibility was illusory and that both could be seen as formulations of the same underlying "fact of mind."[2]

Richards wrote at the height of the influence of logical positivism, and his claim that the two doctrines are in some deep sense equivalent directly reflects that influence. Logical positivism, at the time Richards was writing, was promulgated in England by A. J. Ayer, who maintained that the traditional metaphysical dispute between realism and idealism—as to whether, for instance, a table one perceives has a nature and existence independent of perception or whether it is a construction out of our sensory experiences—wasn't a substantive dispute but, rather, a matter of a "choice" between two different vocabularies, both of which could be used to describe the same underlying facts (which is essentially what Richards maintained). But the principles about language and meaning on which claims like Richards's and Ayer's were based are no longer widely accepted; and my own experience, both in poetry and philosophy, suggests to me that there *is* a question as to whether the impulses central to romanticism have a greater affinity with realism or with its denial. But of course one's understanding of this question depends on what one takes those impulses to be and on what philosophical realism amounts to.

What I take realism, in its basic sense, to be is a thesis to the effect that the world has a determinate character and nature that are independent of our beliefs and thoughts about it, our experience of it, and the concepts with which we seek to describe it. Realism thus insists on a sharp distinction between experience and thought, on the one hand, and the world in which our experience and thought are situated, on the other. At times this distinction can seem to take the form of an estrangement, for, while realism doesn't strictly imply scepticism regarding our knowledge of this independent reality, it is a problem for realism to account for how we are able to arrive at a knowledge of that reality, given its independence from our conception of it. The specter of scepticism is historically one of the principal motivations for denying realism, for by eliminating or blurring the distinction between thought and the world, by refiguring it as in some sense a projection of, or construction out of, our experience, the appearance of a gulf to be bridged between the world and our knowledge of it is erased. This characterization of realism as a view whose central tenet is the mind's independence of or estrangement from the world is, I think, the basic one. Philosophical discussions often frame the issue somewhat differently, as a question of how notions like meaning and truth should be understood—for example, whether a statement's truth depends on the objects (and their properties) to which it refers, regardless of our knowledge of those objects, or whether its truth is ultimately a matter of our rational acceptance of it. There are good reasons, in a technical philosophical context, for reformulating the issue of realism as a semantic one. Here, though, where the question is one of the affinities between realism or its denial and a certain poetic impulse or perspective, I think the original ontological conception of realism is the appropriate one, and this is how I shall understand it. Similarly, though in contemporary philosophical debates the term *antirealism* is often used to refer to specific positive semantic doctrines, I shall use it here simply to refer to any denial of realism as I have characterized it.

The central impulse of romanticism is, I take it, the affirmation of subjectivity. While this affirmation may, in concrete instances, be embodied in or disguised by a championing of individualism, the presentation of the heroic, the picturesque, or the languorous, or the celebration of nature, the underlying movement of romanticism is a contestatory one, in which subjective consciousness seeks to ward off the annihilating effect of its objective setting, a context that is lifeless and inert.

The strategy by which this affirmation is to be achieved is problematic. A straightforward celebration of subjectivity risks collapsing into posturing and vapidity—especially since the contrast between consciousness and its objective setting in the world is liable to make the former appear illusory and a too vigorous insistence upon it an act of delusion. The more likely strategies are indirect, involving a projection through the imagination in which the subjective self is reified or identified with something other or external. This may take the form of personification or the investment of abstractions with subjectivity, as in Milton's allegory of Sin and Death in *Paradise Lost*. It may take of form of animism or the pathetic fallacy, in which nature becomes a mirror for subjective consciousness. It may involve the positing of a quest-object, whose attainment would constitute the self's realization. Or it may take the more complicated form of the sequence of interior movements that Kant called the dynamical sublime, in which the subjective self first feels overwhelmed to the point of extinction by some vast natural presence but is then led, by the realization that it is able to comprehend a presence of this magnitude and to conceive of an even greater and unbounded magnitude not to be found in nature, to posit and identify with a self transcending the natural order.

All these strategies are subject to their own difficulties. Personification risks degenerating into hollow symbolism if the abstractions are rendered too figuratively and into an amorphous vagueness if they are not. The investment of nature with the qualities of consciousness quickly becomes unconvincing and sentimental, while, on the other hand, the object of a quest-romance is liable to appear too external, too lacking in interiority. And the self's identification, in the course of the movements of the sublime, with the transcendental ego posited by the imagination, produces, as Steven Knapp notes, "a mad or comical inflation of the self" that Kant called "fanaticism" or a condition of "rational raving."[3]

Both the issue of realism and the issue of the form romanticism's affirmation of subjectivity should take are thus concerned with the question of how subjective consciousness is seen to be situated in the world, or of what one takes its relation to its objective setting to be. And what I want to consider is whether romanticism's underlying impulse is best implemented in ways that suggest an affinity with the distinction between consciousness and the world posited by realism, on the one hand, or with the blurring of the distinction between them posited by antirealism, on the other.

Stanley Cavell is one of the few philosophers to explore the relationship between philosophical positions and outlooks that would more likely be deemed literary. His main concern is with epistemological scepticism, which he regards as a condition of "despair of the world,"[4] an estrangement that threatens to be a consequence of realism's insistence on the independence of thought and reality. Cavell personifies scepticism in the figure of "the sceptic" and attempts to diagnose the sceptic's rejection of ordinary standards and claims to knowledge. This approach is based on the idea that sceptical arguments are no different in form from arguments we usually find unobjectionable and thus are not open to refutation in any straightforward sense; but that nothing in the concept of knowledge requires that the standards for it be set so high that none of our ordinary beliefs can satisfy them. And this leads us to ask just what attitude towards or relation to the world might be involved in accepting the sceptic's claims:

> My idea is that what in philosophy is known as skepticism . . . is a relation to the world, and to others, and to myself, that is known to what you might call literature, or anyway responded to in literature, in uncounted other guises.[5]

And he takes this relation to be what he calls a refusal of "acknowledgment"—which means, in part, a withdrawal from the everyday forms of life and social practices on which, following Wittgenstein, he takes communication and knowledge to rest.[6]

Responding to scepticism, according to Cavell, involves overcoming an "anxiety about our human capacities as knowers" by recovering what he calls "the prize of the ordinary"—

that is, achieving a sense of an "ordinariness [that] speaks of an intimacy with existence."[7] Such a response is furnished, he maintains, by ordinary language philosophy as practiced by J. L. Austin and others, by American transcendentalism, and by the romanticism of Coleridge and Wordsworth. He takes the fundamental romantic quest to be for the installation of the self *in* the world and the romantic "calling for poetry" to be the attempt to "give the world back, to bring it back, as if to life"—even if that means becoming entangled in the "mysteries of animism" and the pathetic fallacy.[8]

The bases on which Cavell enlists romanticism in this project of the recovery of the ordinary are Wordsworth's professed aim, in the preface to the *Lyrical Ballads,* of rendering "the incidents of common life interesting" and his reading of the Immortality ode. He takes the ode's speaker's address to nature to be a replacement for the more blatant pantheism of the opening stanzas but still a form of expression of an impulse towards the incorporation of the self into the world, or the world into the self. And he regards as an *affirmation* Wordsworth's acknowledgment that the "vision splendid" of "The Soul that rises with us" and that "Hath had elsewhere its setting / And cometh from afar" must ultimately "fade into the light of common day."

This seems to me to confuse the originating impulse of romanticism, which is towards a condition of transcendent subjectivity, with the inevitable recognition that this condition is unsustainable and that it can be achieved, if at all, only in glimpses or intimations. While the child's "exterior semblance doth belie / [The] Soul's immensity," too soon that "Soul shall have her earthly freight / . . . / Heavy as frost, and deep almost as life!" This recognition is not an affirmation but a gesture of resignation or regret—or, if that is too strong (given the last stanza's note of solace), a moment in Wordsworth's characteristic oscillation away from and toward the world, an oscillation so conspicuous also in Stevens. Yet this oscillation is really an attenuation of the movement of the dynamical sublime towards a self transcending the natural order, a movement whose imaginary completion would result in that condition Kant called rational raving. Transcendent subjectivity is thus, for romanticism, an imaginative ideal rather than a condition of actual existence. But this does not mean that its actual impulse is towards a merging with or incorporation into the world, for the price of this incorporation would be a condition of extinction—as in "A Slumber Did My Spirit Seal," where the incorporation of the "thing that could not feel / The touch of earthly years" into nature reduces it to something with no motion or force, which "neither hears nor sees, / Rolled round in earth's diurnal course / With rocks and stones and trees."

I believe that Harold Bloom is right to insist that readings (like Cavell's) that associate Wordsworth, and romanticism generally, with pantheism and a quest for unity with nature are distortions, that the actual relation posited by romanticism between subjectivity and nature is an antagonistic one, and that "Romantic nature poetry, despite a long history of misrepresentation, was an antinature poetry."[9] Wordsworth's achievement, according to Bloom, was to empty poetry of any real content or subject other than pure subjectivity, by making it a field for an internalized quest whose hero is the poet himself, "in a reductive universe of death."[10] And the goal of this internalized quest is not, appearances to the contrary notwithstanding, the recovery of some sort of former union with nature, or the installation of the self in the world, but of a "former selfless self"[11]—which, I take it, is a condition of pure subjectivity, conceptually prior to its objectification in the form of the human person.

Such a condition is of course as unattainable as is the completion of the movement of the dynamical sublime. Yet its status as an unattainable ideal points to the opposition between what Paul de Man calls "the ontological status of the object"[12] and the demands of consciousness. Though romantic poetry manifests, in its language, a *temptation* for "the nostalgia for the object," this temptation actually seeks to thwart the impulse of romanticism; and to see the latter as aspiring to an "unmediated vision" that fuses matter and consciousness in a "happy relation" is to "fail to realize that the very fact that the relationship has to be established within the medium of language indicates that it does not exist in actuality."[13] Invoking

Wordsworth's characterization of nature as a "blank abyss," de Man locates the trajectory of the romantic imagination in an attempt to tear itself away from a terrestrial nature and a movement towards an "other nature . . . associated with the diaphanous, limpid and immaterial quality of a light that dwells nearer to the skies."[14] This is not the conventional imagination of flower imagery but the idea of a savage and self-contained mode of consciousness, capable of existing "entirely by and for itself, independently of all relationship with the outside world, without being moved by an intent aimed at a part of this world."[15] And it is the fascination with some such possibility, unrealizable though it may be, that I take to be the animating force behind the internalized romantic quest.

De Man does acknowledge romanticism's temptation for a movement towards the world that runs counter to this underlying animus. And it is of course undeniable that the tendencies towards merging the self and the world that Cavell mistakenly identifies as romanticism's root impulse are present in its poetry. But I think such tendencies should be seen as a reaction, or countermovement, to the fundamental drive towards the affirmation of subjectivity. That drive tends towards the estrangement of subjectivity from the world, towards the isolation of the subject. But desire is an essential component of subjectivity (at least once it has fallen from that imaginary condition of the "selfless self" to which Bloom thinks it aspires); and a consequence of this withdrawal from the world is that desire remains unfulfilled. Thus the characteristic romantic longing, the impulse of unfulfilled desire, emerges as an inevitable countermovement towards the world—a world of the objects of desire—and the actual trajectory of the romantic imagination isn't de Man's smooth ascension from terrestrial nature but, rather, an oscillatory one, as the basic impulse towards an isolated condition of pure subjectivity is countered by the force of unsatisfied longing it trails in its wake.

The question I posed at the outset was of the relation between theses or positions that are properly philosophical, on the one hand, and, on the other, attitudes or outlooks that aren't really subject to philosophical argument or assessment but which typically inform the operations of the imagination.

Specifically, the question was of the possible affinity between the root impulse of romantic poetry and either philosophical realism or antirealism. My thought was that the existence of such an affinity might both clarify the nature of that impulse and suggest a temperamental or affective dimension to those philosophical positions—and that this might, in turn, help explain what strikes me as the fact that individual philosophers' attractions or aversions to them often seem disproportionate to the strength of the actual arguments for or against them.

If one accepts the idea that what lies at the heart of romanticism is an affirmation of subjectivity, one's first thought would probably be that any affinity it might have with either realism or antirealism would likely be with the latter. Realism emphasizes the independence of the world from our thoughts or conceptions of it, while its denial typically construes the world as in some sense constructed out of subjective experience, or constituted by the beliefs and concepts we form in the course of the human activity of inquiry in the service of the satisfaction of our needs and interests. Antirealism thus seems to magnify or extend the range of the subjective or the human, or to locate the world within the domain of the human—and in doing this it might be thought to affirm the domination of the mind over a setting that would otherwise present an image of its annihilation. But in light of the foregoing account of romanticism, I think that one can see why this appearance of an affinity with antirealism is deceptive. By blurring the distinction between the self and the world, we in effect strip the self of that radical singularity that lies at the heart of the romantic imagination. Blurring the distinction between subjectivity and its objective setting doesn't so much establish its dominion over the latter as allow it to be swallowed up by it. This attempt at a recovery of the world, which Cavell celebrates as an overcoming of scepticism, is part of what I just suggested arises as a countermovement to the impulse of romanticism and threatens a correlative loss of the self as it becomes diminished or extinguished in the fulfillment of its desire for that recovery.

In treating the world as, in some sense, a projection of ourselves and our practices, antirealism challenges our ability to form a conception of a world possessing a character and nature that are independent both of our thoughts or representations of it and of our investigative practices directed towards it— indeed, it is the denial of our ability to form a complete conception of such an independent reality that is characteristic of antirealism in virtually all its forms, including Berkeley's idealism, Richard Rorty's version of pragmatism, Nelson Goodman's irrealism, and Michael Dummett's critique of realism. And for reasons I shall try to bring out momentarily, a central element in the romantic affirmation of subjectivity is the attribution to it of the ability to form a conception of a world radically other than itself.

It may seem paradoxical to associate romanticism's valorization of consciousness with realism's view of the world as essentially inert and discontinuous with the mind, but this is where the affinity lies. The discontinuity may at first seem to diminish or marginalize subjectivity by removing it from the natural order, but I think that this impression is too hasty. The estrangement, in imagination, of consciousness from the world in effect purifies and isolates it, constituting the first step in the severing of its relation to the outside world that gestures towards that "selfless self" and freedom from "terrestrial nature" that Bloom and de Man identify as the basic impulse of romanticism. For in framing a conception of a natural order whose character and nature are independent of our representation of it in thought, one implicitly posits a vantage point or perspective on it that is not a part of that order but transcends it.

Remember the sequence of movements of the dynamical sublime: the apprehension of a physical enormity radically other than the self, by which the self seems diminished; next, the realization that one is able to comprehend that enormity, or contain it in thought; and finally (if carried to its conclusion), the positing of and identification with a transcendental subject of consciousness exempt from the natural world of causality to which the enormity belongs. The world portrayed by realism, it seems to me, amounts to an abstract version of that initially overpowering physical presence. And the mind's ability to form a conception of such a world strikes me as the analogue of the concluding movements of the experience of the sublime that gesture towards a transcendent subjectivity. Sometimes I think that the emblem of both realism and romanticism is that representation of tiny figures in a vast landscape characteristic of Chinese and Dutch landscape painting, in which the human person, externalized and reduced to objective terms, is swallowed up and dwarfed into insignificance— for the very experience of such a representation contains the idea of a subjective position outside that landscape, from which it can be apprehended.

Linking realism to a notion of transcendent subjectivity may seem odd, because realism is usually thought to incorporate, or at least allow for, a materialist position on the mind/body problem that would explain consciousness in natural terms and locate it within the natural realm. I am sceptical about the prospects for such a materialist explanation of consciousness. But whether or not this scepticism is justified is really irrelevant to the issue of romanticism's affinity with realism, for the *idea* of the self as not really part of the world seems to me to be latent in our subjective experience of ourselves; and any materialist account of consciousness and subjectivity would have to accommodate those aspects of our experience that give rise to such an idea. What romanticism requires is the positing by the imagination of an idea of a transcendent subjectivity and a movement or gesturing towards it. But as I've suggested, this movement inevitably gives rise to a countermovement back towards the world. And to insist on the actualization of that idea is to succumb to self-delusion, or to lapse into Kant's condition of rational raving.

One might also object that the conception of the world posited by realism is an unattainable one and that realism itself is an untenable philosophical view. This is in fact one of the main criticisms of realism (though it isn't one I find persuasive). But again, what is at issue here is neither the truth or viability of philosophical realism or the notion of a transcendent subjectivity posited by romanticism but their association. Michael Dummett, one of the most persistent critics of realism, recounts that he once considered an argument for God's existence to the effect that antirealism is incoherent but that realism is only tenable on a theistic basis.[16] Whether realism, theism, or such an argument are ultimately viable is really beside the point. What *is* important is the affinity between a certain philosophical doctrine and a certain way of conceiving of the self's relation to the world that the very idea of such an argument suggests.

This affinity can be seen in the work of many poets of consciousness. Elizabeth Bishop isn't often thought of in this way, but it seems to me that the sense of the subjective viewpoint is as strong in her work as it is in those poets in whom it is rendered more explicitly. Bishop was misconstrued early in her career by critics like M. L. Rosenthal as a passionless and genteel poet whose main strength was the depiction of surfaces but whose work was devoid of the furious sense of self informing the work of contemporaries of hers like Robert Lowell. It *is* true that Bishop's depictive abilities are remarkable; but what is so striking about her work is how she renders objects in a way that isn't merely accurate in a conventional sense but with a clarity that borders on the hallucinatory: a fish's eyes are "packed / with tarnished tinfoil / seen through the lenses / of old scratched isinglass" ("The Fish");[17] "The branches of the date-palms look like files" ("Over 2,000 Illustrations and a Complete Concordance").[18] Consider the stuffed loon in "First Death in Nova Scotia":[19]

> He kept his own counsel
> on his white, frozen lake,
> the marble-topped table.
> His breast was deep and white,
> cold and caressable;
> his eyes were red glass,
> much to be desired.

What this hallucinatory clarity evokes, as much as if not more than the depicted scene itself, is the sense of a subjective vantage point from which that scene is observed and which (as Wittgenstein remarks of the relation of the eye to the visual field) is absent from it. David Kalstone, in his discussion of Bishop's "Quai d'Orleans," notes that what gives her work its power is her "heightened receptiveness . . . to a scene which, in the event, so excludes" the observer.[20] And it is through this almost palpable sense of exclusion permeating her work that subjective consciousness is rendered as an implied presence.

By contrast, in few poets is interiority rendered more explicitly than in Stevens, and in few is its external setting presented more obliquely. The late poems in *The Rock* are suffused, as Helen Vendler has remarked, with the ache of unsatisfied sexual longing.[21] Yet even there Stevens remains stoic in his isolation, gesturing towards the world only to reaffirm his withdrawal from it. "Long and Sluggish Lines" furnishes glimpses of the self's external setting, glimpses that reinforce the self's detachment from it:

> It makes so little difference, at so much more
> Than seventy, where one looks, one has been there before.
>
> Woodsmoke rises through trees, is caught in an upper flow
> Of air and whirled away. But it has often been so.

The world exists as a frame in which the ephemeral seat of the poet's consciousness finds its tenuous location:

> Wanderer, this is the pre-history of February.
> The life of the poem in the mind has not yet begun.
>
> You were not born yet when the trees were crystal
> Nor are you now, in this wakefulness inside a sleep.

"Not Ideas about the Thing but the Thing Itself" flirts with an embrace of reality prompted by unfulfilled desire, but this nostalgia for the object is deflected and transformed. The significance of the external is seen first as its representation in consciousness:

> At the earliest ending of winter,
> In March, a scrawny cry from outside
> Seemed like a sound in his mind.

The poem envisions a "new knowledge of reality"—supplanting "sleep's faded paper mache"—of the sun "coming from outside." But the sun remains "Still far away," and the experience, which is "*like* / A new knowledge of reality" (emph.

added), seems not one of the recovery of the physical world but a second dawn of subjectivity as the poet's life approaches its close.

Nowhere is this sort of reversal, in which an emblem of externality is transformed into an affirmation of interiority, more striking than in "The Rock" itself, which opens with an acknowledgment of the ephemerality, indeed the unreality, of subjectivity:

> It is an illusion that we were ever alive,
> Lived in the houses of mothers, arranged ourselves
> By our own motions in a freedom of air.

But if the self is an illusion, "an impermanence / In its permanent cold," it is "an illusion so desired / That the green leaves came and covered the high rock" of its impersonal, extinguishing context. Ultimately, through the plenitude of the imagination,

> the poem makes meanings of the rock,
> Of such mixed motion and such imagery
> That its barrenness becomes a thousand things
>
> And so exists no more.

As the mind, through the imagination, establishes its dominance over the rock, the latter becomes emblematic of the mind's life (unlike the rocks of "A Slumber Did My Spirit Seal," which become emblems of its extinction). Yet Stevens declines to carry this movement of the sublime toward transcendence to completion, and, as he returns to an acknowledgment of the self's ephemerality, the rock becomes both "The starting point of the human and the end":

> The rock is the gray particular of man's life,
> The stone from which he rises up—and—ho,
> The step to the bleaker depths of his descents.

The rock, transformed into an objectification of man's life, finally takes its true place in "Night's hymn of the rock, as in a vivid sleep."

One reason the issue of realism is cloudy is that neither the purest form of realism nor the purest form of antirealism is a tenable position. An extreme realism divorces the world so entirely from thought that the latter would not even have a role in forming the conceptual categories with which to accurately characterize the world—which makes it difficult to see how we might be able to think about the world at all. An extreme antirealism so merges the world and thought that it becomes hard to explain the obvious fact that through inquiry we seem to discover truths about the world that are not of our own making. Where one situates oneself between these extremes seems to me to some extent to be a question of philosophical temperament and not entirely a matter of argument and rational consideration.

Romanticism, as I have tried to understand it, is similarly torn between a vision of subjectivity as completely *other* than the world and a vision of the world as invested with and constituted by subjectivity. What I have tried to suggest is that romanticism's root affinity is with the first vision and that the second should be seen as a reaction to its austerity and isolation.

We can see this ambivalence in the work of the major romantic poets. Shelley and Wordsworth are both driven, by the apprehension of nature in its enormity and otherness, to a heightened awareness of consciousness. Both of them flirt with the temptation to then invest nature with the qualities of spirit, to project that consciousness upon it. Both are finally sceptical of this investment. And both gesture towards a transcendent vision of the self yet decline to embrace that vision fully and are, in this sense, poets of the attenuated sublime. Shelley's "Mont Blanc" opens as "The everlasting universe of things / Flows through the mind" and proceeds to a recognition of the mind's estrangement from it:

> Dizzy Ravine! And when I gaze on thee
> I seem as in a trance sublime and strange
> To muse on my own separate fantasy,
> My own, my human mind.

Mont Blanc is a site from which the human is absent—

                              the snows descend
          Upon that Mountain; none beholds them there

—yet the poet still ascribes to it a "secret Strength of things /
Which governs thought" and renders the mountain knowable.
But the final image of the poem, which takes the form of a
question, is of a nature that is inconceivable in its estrange-
ment from consciousness:

          And what were thou, and earth, and stars, and sea,
          If to the human mind's imaginings
          Silence and solitude were vacancy?

   Wordsworth's recollection—or perception—of the world is
one of such tenderness that at times it can almost seem—and
seem to him—to have been created by his imagination or
apprehension of it, as at the conclusion of book 12 of *The
Prelude:*

                                     I remember well
               That in life's everyday appearances
               I seemed about this period to have sight
               Of a new world, a world, too, that was fit
               To be transmitted and made visible
               To other eyes, having for its base
               That whence our dignity originates,
               That which both gives it being and maintains
               A balance, an ennobling interchange
               Of action from within and from without:
               The excellence, pure spirit, and best power
               Both of the object seen, and the eye that sees.

But the concluding vision of *The Prelude* exhibits the affinity
that I've argued exists between the romantic affirmation of
subjective consciousness and the conception of a world from
which that consciousness is estranged—a magisterial vision of

               how the mind of man becomes
          A thousand times more beautiful than the earth
          On which he dwells, above this Frame of things.

Here the human figure is installed in the natural order. Yet the perspective that the human mind is able to take on that order *seems* to allow it to transcend it, to bestow on the mind an existence "above this Frame of things"—a frame of *things* (whatever their natures may be) that are independent of us, indifferent to us, and which lie at the heart of realism's conception of the world. And this, it seems to me, is romanticism's fundamental way of imagining the relation of the self to the world.

## NOTES

1. I. A. Richards, *Coleridge on Imagination* (New York: Norton, 1950), 145.

2. Richards, *Coleridge on Imagination*, 147.

3. Steven Knapp, *Personification and the Sublime* (Cambridge: Harvard University Press, 1985), 3.

4. Stanley Cavell, *In Quest of the Ordinary* (Chicago: University of Chicago Press, 1988), 4.

5. Ibid., 154–55.

6. Cavell, "Knowing and Acknowledging," in *Must We Mean What We Say* (New York: Scribner's, 1969).

7. Cavell, *In Quest of the Ordinary*, 4.

8. Ibid., 44–45.

9. Harold Bloom, "The Internalization of Quest-Romance," in *Romanticism and Consciousness*, ed. Harold Bloom (New York: Norton, 1970), 9.

10. Ibid., 8.

11. Ibid., 16.

12. Paul de Man, "Intentional Structure of the Romantic Image," in Bloom, *Romanticism and Consciousness*, 70.

13. Ibid., 70.

14. Ibid., 75.

15. Ibid., 76–77.

16. Michael Dummett, *Truth and Other Enigmas* (Cambridge: Harvard University Press, 1978), xxxix.

17. In Elizabeth Bishop, *The Complete Poems, 1927–1979* (New York: Farrar, Straus and Giroux, 1983).

18. Ibid.

19. Ibid.

20. David Kalstone, *Becoming a Poet* (New York: Farrar, Straus and Giroux, 1989), 67.

21. Helen Vendler, "Apollo's Harsher Songs," *Part of Nature, Part of Us* (Cambridge: Harvard University Press, 1980).

# Poetry at One Remove
## (1998)

The installation of poets in the academy is now so complete that it is easy to forget that the relation of poetry and contemporary literature—let alone poets and contemporary writers—to departments of literature was once considered problematic. It was not really until the establishment of the New Criticism that contemporary poetry became an acceptable object of academic literary studies, and even then the methods of reading it applied, and the readings of the works of high modernism those methods yielded, tended to ignore issues of authorial presence and of the ways in which works of literature were actually produced. True, most of the major poets of the generation succeeding the high modernists—Delmore Schwartz, Robert Lowell, John Berryman, Randall Jarrell, Elizabeth Bishop—spent at least parts of their careers in English departments. But more often than not this was as teachers and scholars of literature, as with Berryman and Schwartz, or, as with Lowell and Bishop, as individual teachers of writing, whose roles were sui generis and left them only distantly connected to the departments to which they were formally attached. It is only recently, with the explosion in the number of creative writing programs, that the idea of poetry as the basis of an entire academic career has emerged, a career in which one receives formal instruction in the writing of poetry both as an undergraduate and as a graduate student and, having thus acquired the requisite credentials, joins the professoriate in a capacity structurally no different from that of a professor of German, philosophy, or economics.

My own situation as a poet has always placed me at one remove from formal literary studies and the teaching of writ-

From *New Literary History* 30, no. 1 (winter 1999). Reprinted by permission.

ing. In high school I was deeply fascinated by literature, particularly modernist fiction, and did a certain amount of writing myself. But these were secondary to my primary interests in mathematics and physics, which I intended to pursue as a career. In college my interest shifted to philosophy, and I began writing poetry seriously. At that time there were at Princeton a number of undergraduate poets, most of them (even those who were English majors) united in their disdain for the English department and the contemporary poets of whom its faculty approved. R. P. Blackmur did serve as a source of encouragement and inspiration, though of course he was himself an autodidact whose relationship to academia was a somewhat uneasy one. Several little magazines were edited on the campus, some with ties to poets of the New York School, and discussions of poetry were usually intense exercises in what nowadays would be called theory. As a graduate student in philosophy at Harvard, I found the relation of students who were poets to the university to be different, with a much greater sense of allegiance to the institution and to the writers associated with it. I found this atmosphere uncongenial and came to think of my role in the university almost entirely in terms of my philosophical studies while associating myself as a writer with the poets and artists I knew in New York, in the completely uninstitutional setting of the small part of the literary world they constituted there. And I have continued to think of my role as a philosopher as a professional and academic one and of the writing of poetry as at some level an essentially gratuitous act. And, while it may be making a virtue of necessity, I have a vague feeling that this sense of estrangement from the idea of writing as an academic profession is not entirely disadvantageous and that it has had a distinctive effect on the way in which I think of poetry and on the actual poetry I write. At least that is what I want to try to explore here.

There are certainly incidental effects of coming to poetry from outside the arena of literary studies and of coming to it from the practice of philosophy in particular. There is a kind of orthodoxy in contemporary poetry that favors the concrete, the vivid, the evocative, and the particular and avoids the discursive and the abstract. I think that it is possible to endow the sort of theoretical reflection associated, at least in the popular mind, with philosophy with considerable emotional resonance—indeed, this is one of my primary poetic aims. The discursive and the abstract are philosophy's stock in trade, and a background in the discipline tends to make one at ease with these rhetorical modes. Eliot was one of the few poets trained in philosophy, and this manifests itself in the assurance with which he ventures into the realm of abstraction and the way in which his use of the conceptional idiom always seems casual and matter-of-fact, even at its most rarified. Stevens, by contrast, though often thought of as a philosophical poet, had no formal training in the discipline. And I think that this may be part of the reason why the language of his ruminations, usually so magnificent in its suppleness and profusion, occasionally seems a bit forced, as though he were trying to inhabit a rhetorical mode in which he was not entirely at home. This is not to say that a background in philosophy enables one to bring the conceptual methods of the discipline to bear on poetry. Meditation and speculation in philosophy are subject to severe constraints—this is, in a way, its point—whereas the movement of the mind in poetry is essentially *un*constrained. And I think that an important consequence of having an identity as a poet that is not institutionally validated is that this freedom from conceptual constraint, which lies at the heart of the conception of poetry I hold, is reinforced and enhanced.

No doubt there are also incidental effects, some of them detrimental, on poetry written in the role of a literary scholar or a teacher of writing. The latter role is especially liable to have an adverse effect on one's work, since the fact that the poetry written in that role bears essentially the same relation to one's career and livelihood as does the writing of anyone in academia certainly has the potential to render it, over the course of time, formulaic and tired, issuing not from an impulse internal to the poetic act but from pressures external to it. Yet of course many poets who teach writing for a living manage to avoid these kinds of dangers, which in any case do not strike me as terribly interesting, being only externally related to poetic practice. What does interest me is the question of whether having an identity as a poet that does not coincide with an institutionally constituted role might have conceptual consequences internal to the poetic impulse itself, affecting the character of the relation between the authorial self or subject and the poetry that issues from that site.

The conception of poetry that animates my work is based on what I take to be the fundamental impulse underlying romanticism: the enactment and affirmation of subjectivity and the contestation of its inert, objective setting in a world that is emblematic of its annihilation. As I have described it in several essays in this book, the idea of subjectivity informing this conception is of a self not part of the real and objective world at all, a pure and impersonal subject of interiority prior to its objectification in the form of an actual person. It is in this sense a transcendental notion, though putting it this way verges on the delusional inflation of the self Kant called "fanaticism" and "rational raving."[1] It is better, I think, to think of it as a necessary illusion or fiction, a fiction to be enacted and affirmed in spite of the knowledge that it *is* a fiction. And one form this enactment takes is the representation of an attenuated version of the experience Kant, in the *Critique of Judgement,* called the dynamical sublime, in which the self, at first threatened by its perception of a world that reduces it to insignificance, attempts to attain a vantage point from which that world can be encompassed in thought.[2]

The situation of the romantic authorial self is in some ways a paradoxical one. On the one hand, it is bound to poetic practice by a sense of obligation or duty, an obligation to realize in language the abstract idea or form of the poem it is attempting to inscribe. On the other hand, that poem is something that does not yet exist to impose its demands on the poet, and the act of bringing it into existence is felt to be an exercise of unconstrained creation, an expression of subjectivity's freedom from externally imposed constraints that lies at the heart of the romantic imagination. Thus the notion of an obligation that is freely self-imposed is central to the conception of the genuine poetic act, and this odd combination of freedom and duty is again reminiscent of Kant, this time of his moral philosophy. Kant thought that the duties making up what he called the moral law flowed from the single formal principle that one must freely constrain one's conduct to accord with principles applicable to all rational beings. He may have been too optimistic in this: most interpreters of Kant doubt that substantive moral obligations can be derived solely from the formal principle he called the categorical imperative. In her important recent book *The Sources of Normativity*[3] Christine Korsgaard argues that in order to arrive at substantive duties incumbent on a person the categorical imperative has to be supplemented with assumptions about that person's *practical identity*, by which she means the self-conception he has adopted to define the kind of person he takes himself to be. *Practical* here is a theoretical term. A person's practical identity as, say, a mother sets limits on her actions, for since certain actions are at odds with this identity *she* cannot freely choose to do them, for if she were to act in these ways she would not be the kind of person she is. There are a variety of practical identities a person might adopt: as a mother, as a member of an ethnic or religious group, as a member of a certain profession, and so on. *Moral* obligations are those flowing from one's practical identity as merely a human being, as a member of "the party of humanity,"[4] an identity that it is in a way futile to resist acknowledging, since that is what, in the last analysis, one essentially is.

It strikes me that Korsgaard's version of Kantianism, with its notion of a chosen practical identity, helps make sense of the idea of freely self-imposed poetic obligation I take to be so central to the genuine poetic process. In adopting a practical identity as a poet, one obligates one's self to a poetic practice consonant with that identity. Yet as long as that identity is freely—even gratuitously—chosen, the obligations flowing from it are self-imposed and conformity to them a manifestation, rather than a limitation, of the freedom underlying the poetic act. Just as a range of practical identities are open to one, so there are a variety of poetic identities one might adopt, in particular those underlying what might be thought of as the poetics of a limited identity, in which one's work attempts to embody the perspective of some group, class, gender, or sexual identity, or, as in confessional poetry, of some actual individual. But if one conceives of poetry as I do, as an enactment of pure subjectivity, these kinds of poetic identities are liable to seem evasions of one's fundamental poetic identity as a locus of self-reflective consciousness—just as the adoption of a practical identity as a member of an ethnic group can be an evasion of one's basic practical identity as a member of the party of humanity. Indeed, since self-reflective consciousness is what is distinctive of human beings, it might seem that a poetic identity as a locus of pure subjectivity and a practical identity as a human being are one and the same, and it seems to me that an intriguing way of thinking about high Wordsworthian romanticism is to see it as trying to equate a poetic identity with an identity as a member of the party of humanity and so merging the aesthetic and the moral. But just as the full version of the experience of Kant's dynamical sublime is not really open to us, the only form of romanticism tenable now is a truncated and belated one, which enacts the claims of a transcendent subjectivity while at the same time acknowledging it to be illusory and which defines the poetic self by opposing it to the objective world to which we, as actual human beings, belong.

Central to my conception of poetry, then, is the notion of a freely assumed poetic identity as a subject of self-reflective consciousness, an authorial self that attempts to enact and portray that subjectivity in one's work. But if one's identity as a poet is institutionally constituted and sanctioned, one's relation to that work becomes problematic. It is essential that the relation between the poet and his work be an internal one between a freely adopted authorial self and a poetry that enacts that self's subjective consciousness—for only in that way can conformity to the obligations that relation engenders manifest the sense of freedom that lies at the heart of the romantic imagination of the self. But if one's poetic identity is in part a matter of an institutional role one occupies, there is always a danger that one will come to see it as externally imposed—in which case the relation between the authorial self and the work that flows from it will be altered. The work will no longer seem to be created in conformity to a self-imposed obligation but in conformity to a duty imposed from the outside. And this is liable to affect the character of the poetic act itself. Let me adapt and alter slightly an example of Bernard Williams's concerning moral deliberation to illustrate the point. A man's wife is drowning, and he acts, with some risk to himself, to save her, which is what morality requires of him. Were his deliberation to include the thought that he must save her *because she is his wife,* he surely would have, as Williams puts it, "one thought too many."[5] What would be objectionable here is the fact that his moral impulse would be mediated by the thought of a duty he has by virtue of the socially constituted relation he bears to her. He does, of course, *have* this externally imposed duty. But the idea of the thought of it intruding into his process of moral reflection seems repugnant. Similarly, the thought that one assumes a poetic identity *because it is part of one's job* seems foreign to the relation that should hold between the poet and his work. Of course assuming such an identity may indeed be required by one's institutionally defined role, and one may nevertheless assume it freely, unaffected by the thought that one is required to do so. But if such an externally imposed duty is in fact incumbent upon one, it is liable in practice to be difficult to resist having an awareness of it enter into the poetic process, thereby altering the character of that process.

But if one writes outside of the context of an institutional role that defines one as a poet, then the assumption of a poetic identity as an articulator of self-reflective subjectivity can only be freely assumed, since one is under no externally imposed obligation to assume it. There is an existential overtone here (as there is, I think, to Korsgaard's version of Kantianism): what makes the poetic process authentic is the fact that it proceeds from a freely chosen identity, rather, that from an identity one finds one's self to have. In fact, the whole conception of poetry I hold has an existential cast to it, for it insists on the affirmation of a subjectivity that is acknowledged not to be part of the objective natural order and in that sense not factual or real. And it is only on this conception of poetry that the occupation of an institutionally defined role as a poet threatens the integrity of the poetic process. If one conceives of poetry in other terms—formally, culturally, confessionally, or linguistically—one need not take one's poetic identity to be a locus of unconstrained subjective consciousness. Indeed, some conceptions of poetry do not presuppose a particular conception of poetic identity at all. And most academic disciplines presuppose no particular idea of the self. There is no tension between, say, doing philosophy and being a professional academic philosopher, because philosophy is standardly conceived in terms of certain institutionally sanctioned texts, issues, problems, and methods, rather than as an activity to which the self bears an internal relation. If one thinks of philosophy differently, though, then professionalism *can* seem a threat to its practice. Wittgenstein thought of philosophy not in terms of texts and problems but as the continuing struggle of the mind "against the bewitchment of our intelligence by means of language"[6] and of "the real discovery" as "The one that gives philosophy peace, so that it is no longer tormented by questions which bring *itself* in question."[7] And he also famously loathed the company of academic philosophers and attempted to convince his best students not to pursue the discipline as a professional career, because of the threat this would pose to their intellectual and spiritual integrity.

Yet there is something problematic about insisting on a distinction between the authorial self as a locus of pure subjectivity and the practical identity one has by virtue of a role one happens to occupy—a difficulty that is an instance of the more general problem of the relation between the authorial self and the actual person one happens to be and which emerges at the level of poetry's content. Subjectivity, even in a purely impersonal form, is intrinsically perspectival, since it can be grasped only from the first-person perspective each of us occupies. A poetry that attempts to enact and embody it, then, will almost inevitably be a poetry of the first person. Yet since one is of course a particular person, with a particular personality, a particular history, character, and temperament, and with particular relationships to other people, why, if one writes a poetry of the first person that is not simply devoid of content, will not the self of that poetry collapse into that actual personality? And if it does, rather than an enactment of subjectivity *simpliciter,* will it not collapse into a confessional poetry of the concrete individual voice, with all the (to my mind retrograde) literary, theoretical, and political connotations this kind of poetry is usually taken to have?

The problem is that there is really no such thing as a self that is simply a locus of pure subjectivity *simpliciter;* yet there *is* a poetry that is animated the idea of this kind of self. One might try to evade the difficulty by renouncing the poetry of the first person altogether. But given subjectivity's essentially perspectival character, this would yield at best a truncated view of the interior. Or one might simply omit any reference to the personal or try to invest it with an ironic character that keeps it at arm's length. These strategies are not very satisfactory either—the first tends to yield to a poetry that seems either evasive or preciously thin and the second a poetry that seems smug and condescending. What I have tried to do in my own work—I cannot say with how much success—is to reimagine the first person by simply acquiescing in its poetry and incorporating the materials of personal life when the movement of the poem tends in that direction but enveloping them in a language that is dry, abstract, and matter-of-fact, yet with an insistent lyric undertone. The self of the poem is thus rendered in a way that seems factually adequate but which presents it as a partially fictitious entity, slightly off-center and out of focus, leaving the reader with a sense of a difference between the person of the poem and the authorial site from which the poem emanates, a sense of which I hope the reader is not entirely conscious.

The problem with the poetry of the concrete individual voice is that its demand for fidelity to the experience of the actual self is the internal analogue of the constraint resulting from an externally imposed practical poetic identity: both represent limitations on the freedom of the self of transcendent subjectivity and hinder the enactment of a poetry that embodies that conception of the self. One can escape the constraint of an externally imposed or institutionally sanctioned poetic identity simply by failing to have one; but the demand of fidelity to one's actual experience cannot be avoided so easily, since one cannot fail to be an actual person. I think the solution is not to either ignore or confront the conventional poetry of the first person but, rather, to acquiesce in its outward form while at the same time fleshing out that form through a process that is self-reflexively aware of its distance from the experience being described, so that in the end one stands to the seemingly confessional poem that results in something like the relation Borges's Pierre Menard stands to *Don Quixote:* the novel he writes is indistinguishable from Cervantes', yet it is a different work, and a work of a different character from Cervantes', because of the peculiarly self-conscious character of the process that produced it. When Eliot says in "East Coker" that "The poetry does not matter," one thing he means is that a poem is significant not so much as a verbal artifact but as a manifestation of the process—"the intolerable wrestle / With words and meanings"—by which it comes into existence.[8] And the poetic process underlying the conception of poetry I hold is one that insists on its freedom from the constraints of an externally imposed practical identity and from the internal demands of one's actual experience.

It might be felt that the notion of a transcendent subject of experience, of a self that is the locus of pure, unconstrained subjectivity, is an untenable one and that this vitiates any conception of poetry that incorporates that notion. This seems to me backwards. One does not decide on theoretical grounds whether to be engaged by a particular kind of poetry—to do so would be comparable to adopting a religious outlook because one had been persuaded, say, that the modal version of the ontological argument was valid. Rather, one simply finds oneself compelled by poetry of a particular sort and then acquiesces in the conception of the self that informs that poetry, even in the full knowledge that that conception of the self is illusory. A comparison might be with the status I take philosophical dualism to have. In its current form the mind-body problem basically amounts to the attempt to provide a materialist account of consciousness. Though I cannot give a conclusive argument for it, I have a strong intuition that because of the perspectival character of consciousness it is not possible to provide such an account. Instead, something about the character of our own reflective self-experience makes us unable to avoid thinking of ourselves as immaterial Cartesian egos, even though we may also be convinced that this conception of the self is untenable or even incoherent. Dualism thus has the status of a kind of necessary illusion, an unsatisfactory view to which we are unable to find any satisfactory alternative. Unlike dualism, the conception of the poetic self I have been describing is not a universal illusion, since, while everyone has the kind of reflective self-experience that gives rise to dualism, not everyone is engaged by poetry, let alone by the particular kind of poetry that engages me. But if one *is* engaged by poetry of this kind, then one will almost inevitably have a conception of the authorial self as a locus of transcendent, unconstrained subjectivity. That one acknowledges this conception to be illusory only makes one's willing acquiescence in it an even stronger enactment of it. As Stevens, our greatest poet of pure subjectivity, characteristically put it, "The final belief is to believe in a fiction, which you know to be a fiction, there being nothing else. The exquisite truth is to know that it is a fiction and you believe in it willingly."[9]

There is a temptation to read statements like this as expressions of the aestheticism for which Stevens is sometimes faulted. But I see them as an insistence on the autonomy of the authorial self, an autonomy which involves a freedom even from the demand of fidelity to the factual. It is worth remembering that a similar insistence on the self's autonomy lies at the heart of Kant's ethics, and far from taking Stevens to be espousing a kind of precious aestheticism, I see him, both in his work and in his reflections on the poetic process, as representing a poetic integrity possessing an almost moral weight.

The parallel with Kant's ethics may also help clarify what I have been trying to suggest about the relationship between the poet and the professional academy. Kant is sometimes taken to hold that, since to act morally is to act from the motive of duty, a person cannot act morally if he derives any pleasure or benefit from his action. But of course it is possible for one's motivation to be moral even if one happens to take pleasure in an action one performs from that motive. Similarly, nothing I have said is meant to suggest that occupying a professional role as a writer is somehow incompatible with writing from a genuine poetic impulse or that writing from outside such a role somehow endows the work one produces with a special distinction. I have been arguing for an internal or conceptual connection between a certain neoromantic conception of poetry and the idea of a freely assumed poetic identity, an identity that is a necessary though not a sufficient condition for the successful enactment of poetry of that kind. Whether one is able to combine such a freely chosen identity with an externally sanctioned professional identity, or whether the latter is liable to displace the former, depends, I believe, on a poet's contingent psychological makeup and temperament. There are certainly accomplished poets who are able to combine the two roles—perhaps because they are able to so compartmentalize them that they really have little to do with each other or perhaps because their roles as teachers of writing are simply extensions of their identities as poets and only incidentally professional. I can only say that in my own case I have found the sense of a disjunction between my identity as a poet and my academic role as a philosopher to be a strangely liberating one, engendering in me a conviction that, at least for those of a certain temperament and cast of mind, poetry may sometimes be engaged most intimately when it is engaged at one remove.

## NOTES

1. Quoted without reference by Steven Knapp in *Personification and the Sublime* (Cambridge: Harvard University Press, 1985), 3.

2. Immanuel Kant, *Critique of Judgement,* trans. Werner S. Pluhar (Indianapolis: Hackett, 1987), pt. 1, bk. 2, secs. 28–29.

3. Christine Korsgaard, *The Sources of Normativity* (Cambridge: Cambridge University Press, 1996), chap. 3.

4. Ibid., 118.

5. Bernard Williams, "Persons, Character and Morality," *Moral Luck* (Cambridge: Cambridge University Press, 1981), 18.

6. Ludwig Wittgenstein, *Philosophical Investigations,* 3d. ed., trans. G. E. M. Anscombe (New York: Macmillan, 1968), sec. 109.

7. Ibid., sec. 133.

8. T. S. Eliot, "East Coker," *The Complete Poems and Plays, 1909–1950* (New York: Harcourt, Brace and World, 1952), ll. 71–72.

9. Quoted without reference by Roger Kimball in "A Metaphysical Loss Adjuster," *TLS,* no. 4946, Jan. 16, 1998, 29.

UNDER DISCUSSION
David Lehman, General Editor
Donald Hall, Founding Editor

Volumes in the Under Discussion series collect reviews and essays about individual poets. The series is concerned with contemporary American and English poets about whom the consensus has not yet been formed and the final vote has not been taken. Titles in the series include: